ISSUES IN POLITICAL THEORY

Political Theory has undergone a remarkable development in recent years. From a state in which it was once declared dead, it has come to occupy a central place in the study of Politics. Both political ideas and the wide-ranging arguments to which they give rise are now treated in a rigorous, analytical fashion, and political theorists have contributed to disciplines as diverse as economics, sociology and law. These developments have made the subject more challenging and exciting, but they have also added to the difficulties of students and others coming to the subject for the first time. Much of the burgeoning literature in specialist books and journals is readily intelligible only to those who are already well-versed in the subject.

Issues in Political Theory is a series conceived in response to this situation. It consists of a number of detailed and comprehensive studies of issues central to Political Theory which take account of the latest developments in scholarly debate. While making original contributions to the subject, books in the series are written especially for those who are new to Political Theory. Each volume aims to introduce its readers to the intricacies of a fundamental political issue and to help them find their way through the detailed, and often complicated, argument that this issue has attracted.

PETER JONES
ALBERT WEALE

ISSUES IN POLITICAL THEORY

Series editors: PETER JONES and ALBERT WEALE

Published

Forthcoming

Social Contract

Michael Lessnoff

HUMANITIES PRESS INTERNATIONAL, INC.
ATLANTIC HIGHLANDS, NJ

First published in 1986 in the United States of America by
HUMANITIES PRESS INTERNATIONAL, INC., Atlantic Highlands, NJ 07716

LIBRARY OF CONGRESS CATALOGING IN PUBLICATION DATA

Lessnoff, Michael H. (Michael Harry)
   Social contract.
   (Issues in political theory)
   Bibliography; p.
   Includes index.
   1. Social contract—History. I. Title. II. Series.
JC336.L47   1986   320.1'1   86-7189
ISBN 0-391-03436-7
ISBN 0-391-03435-9 (pbk.)

PRINTED IN HONG KONG

Contents

Preface and Acknowledgements

It is a pleasure to acknowledge debts of gratitude incurred in the writing of this book. First mention must go to the series editors, Peter Jones and Albert Weale, but for whom it would not have been written, while Steven Kennedy of Macmillan has been an exemplary publisher. I am grateful to my Glasgow colleagues Mary Haight, Chris Berry, John Fowler, Andrew Lockyer and Fred Hay for reading the typescript in whole or in part, and giving me the benefit of their more expert knowledge in several areas. In particular, John Fowler convinced me that my account of feudalism needed correction; likewise, I have amended some remarks on Rousseau in the light of criticisms by Peter Jones. Discussion with Dudley Knowles helped me to clarify some of my ideas. I have also benefited by a useful exchange with Quentin Skinner on Salamonio, by advice from John Sanderson on seventeenth-century political ideas, and by help from David Raphael, Bill Lyons, Stephen Clark, Stephen White and Joe Houston. The production of the typescript itself, surmounting the severe problems presented by my microscopic handwriting, was the work of Barbara Fisher, Avril Johnstone and Elspeth Shaw, and I am grateful to them also. But my greatest debt of gratitude is to Mary Haight, for reading the entire typescript, giving invaluable help with the understanding of Latin sources, and general encouragement. I should like to dedicate this book to her.

Finally I should like to explain the usage I have adopted in this book in relation to gender. The English language, unfortunately, does not possess suitably neutral third person singular pronouns and adjectives, and thus forces a choice between masculine and feminine ones, even where the meaning makes this inappropriate, if one is to avoid clumsy formulations such as 'he or she'.

Feminists, understandably, have objected to the long-established tradition of using the masculine form to refer to members of the human race as such. Nevertheless, I have, despite reservations, adhered to the traditional practice; not, I hasten to assure the reader, out of sexism or insensitivity, but for reasons of euphony and style, at least as they appear to my ear.

Michael Lessnoff

Explanation of References

The system of referencing used in this book is somewhat complicated, being a compromise between the needs of scholarship and those of publishing. There are three types of references, as follows:

1. Major and classic references are indicated in parenthesis in the text, by means of a capital letter or letters followed by the page number(s) or, occasionally, the number of a chapter. These reference letters are listed and explained below.
2. Other single references are given according to the Harvard system, that is, once again parenthetically in the text, but by citing author's name and year of publication before page number(s). Full bibliographical details of texts referred to can be found at the end of the book. Where the same text figures in successive references, author and year are given only in the first case.
3. Multiple references, references with comments, and additional explanatory material are given in the Notes, indicated in the text by the usual superscript figures.

List of reference letters

B & T   J. M. Buchanan and G. Tullock, *The Calculus of Consent* (University of Michigan Press, 1965)

CIII   A. J. Carlyle, *Medieval Political Theory in the West*, III (London: Blackwood, 1915)

F   R. Filmer, *Patriarcha and Other Political Works*, ed. P. Laslett (Oxford: Blackwell, 1949)

GMA   O. Gierke, *Political Theories of the Middle Age* (Cambridge University Press, 1900)

GNL   O. Gierke, *Natural Law and the Theory of Society, 1500–1800* (Cambridge University Press, 1934)

GPT   O. Gierke, *The Development of Political Theory* (London: Allen & Unwin, 1939)

HC   T. Hobbes, *De Cive or the Citizen* (New York: Appleton-Century-Crofts, 1949)

HH   G. W. F. Hegel, *Lectures on the Philosophy of History* (London: Bohm's Philosophical Library, 1872)

HL   T. Hobbes, *Leviathan* (Harmondsworth: Penguin, 1968)

HN   G. W. F. Hegel, *Natural Law* (University of Pennsylvania Press, 1975)

HR   G. W. F. Hegel, *Philosophy of Right* (Oxford: Clarendon Press, 1952)

HTP   D. Hume, *Theory of Politics*, ed. F. Watkins (Edinburgh: Nelson, 1951)

K   I. Kant, *Kant's Political Writings*, ed. H. Reiss (Cambridge University Press, 1977)

L   J. Locke, *Second Treatise of Government and A Letter Concerning Toleration* (Oxford: Blackwell, 1966)

LDL   H. Laski (ed.), *A Defence of Liberty against Tyrants* (London: Bell, 1924) – a reprint of the 1689 English translation of the *Vindiciae Contra Tyrannos*

N   R. Nozick, *Anarchy, State, and Utopia* (Oxford: Blackwell, 1974)

P   E. B. Pashukanis, 'Theory of Law and Marxism', in H. W. Babb and J. N. Hazard, *Soviet Legal Philosophy*, (Harvard University Press, 1951)

PJA   *The Politics of Johannes Althusius*, abridged by F. S. Carney (London: Eyre & Spottiswood, 1965)

PJN   S. Pufendorf, *De Jure Naturae et Gentium*, translated by C. H. and W. A. Oldfather (Oxford: Clarendon Press, 1934)

POH   S. Pufendorf, *De Officio Hominis et Civis*, translated by F. G. Moore (New York: Oxford University Press, 1927)

R   J.-J. Rousseau, *The Social Contract and Discourses* (London: Dent, 1973)

RJ   J. Rawls, *A Theory of Justice* (Harvard University Press, 1971)

S   M. Salamonio, *De Principatu* (Milan: Giuffre Editore, 1955)

1 Introductory

In recent decades the theory of social contract, long thought by many to be by now of purely historical interest, has enjoyed a spectacular rebirth. Primarily this has been a phenomenon of political and moral philosophy, yet it has manifested itself too at the level of practical politics. 'At the heart of our programme to save the nation lies the Social Contract'; these are the words of the manifesto published by the British Labour Party just before its victory in the election of October 1974[1] – the second general election of that year. It was a year that saw sharp economic and political crisis in Britain and elsewhere, which the redemptionist language of the manifesto reflects. In this crisis the nation was to look for its salvation to the social contract.

Subsequent events hardly justified such high hopes. Nor was Labour's social contract quite the same thing as the concept that dominated western political philosophy for centuries, and which will be our concern in this book – nor could one expect it to be, multifarious though the philosophical concept has itself been. The Labour Party 'contract' was between the Labour Government and one section of society, the trade union movement – a good deal of society was, after all, missing from this social contract. Again, the Labour Party's social contract was, obviously, a specific programme for political action rather than a theory designed to explain and evaluate political life in general. But in spite of all this, the social contract of the Labour manifesto is of the greatest interest, as an indication of the continuing popular resonance of the idea, however vaguely understood, and of its felt appropriateness, in some quarters at least, as a foundation of politics in difficult times. The social contract idea is part of our heritage.

If one were asked to explain this phenomenon, in all probability it is to the philosophical tradition that one should turn, and above all to one book in particular – Jean-Jacques Rousseau's *Du*

1

Contrat Social, first published in 1762, just over a quarter of a century before the great French Revolution. Everyone who knows anything of history or political theory knows of Rousseau's *Social Contract*. Rousseau's book is indeed the culmination of one major phase of the social contract tradition – of its most recent phase, prior to the present renaissance – and is typical of it in some ways, though not in all. It is typical in this central respect, that it offers an analysis of *political authority* in terms of a contract involving those subject to that authority. 'Man was born free; and everywhere he is in chains . . . what can make [this] legitimate?' asks Rousseau in the famous opening words of his first chapter. Rousseau's answer is – the social contract, or rather his version of it. The terms of legitimate political authority are the terms of this contract. Indeed, so *political* is the significance of the contract that its traditional name, used by Rousseau – the *social* contract – is a little misleading; 'political contract' would be a better term. At all events, this conception provides me with an operational definition of social contract theory, as a focus for the discussion in this book; a social contract theory is a theory in which a contract is used to justify and/or to set limits to political authority, or in other words, in which political obligation is analysed as a contractual obligation. Admittedly this definition is too narrow to cover the most recent phase of social contract theory, but it will serve well enough for the earlier phases, and its precise meaning should become clearer as we undertake a detailed discussion of the latter – a task on which we shall soon embark.

Before that, however, we need some sharper analysis of the concept of contract. Contract is a legal term, and the notion of the social or political contract postulates that political obligation is analogous to the legal obligation of a party to a contract. It must be stressed that this is an analogy, not an identity – it is not postulated by contract theorists that political obligation *is* a legal obligation. Indeed, since the function of social contract theory is to give an account of politically organised society ('civil society', as many theorists have called it), and civil law is itself one aspect of the latter, it would be manifestly absurd to base political obligation on law in this sense. Clearly it must rest on something prior to civil law; and the typical understanding of contract theorists has been that the contractual obligation they postulate is founded on *natural* law. To this we shall return; but in the meantime we must see what light law in the ordinary sense sheds on the notion of contract.

According to an authoritative legal textbook, a contract (between two parties) 'is an agreement intended to create and actually creating' a right of one party against the other.

'It commonly takes the form of a promise or a set of promises. That is to say, a declaration of the consenting wills of two persons that one of them shall henceforth be under an obligation to the other naturally assumes the form of an undertaking by the one with the other to fulfil the obligation so created. Not every promise however, amounts to a contract. To constitute a contract there must be not merely a promise to do a certain act, but a promise, express or implied, to do this act as a legal duty. . . . The essential form of a contract is not: I promise this to you; but: I agree with you that henceforth you shall have a legal right to demand and receive this from me.' (Williams, 1957, p.385)

Thus, roughly speaking, a legal contract is constituted by a promise, but not by a promise alone, for also required is agreement between the parties that the promise be legally enforceable. Interpreting social contract theory by analogy with this conception, the political obligation with which the theory deals would also be constituted by a promise but, as already explained, there can be no question of agreement that it be *legally* enforceable. Nevertheless, the analogy does not collapse at this point. The social contract, too, is not constituted by a promise alone, for even if legal enforcement is irrelevant, enforcement as such is not, and the understanding that the contract is enforceable is part of its essence.

In one respect the above definition of contract is a little surprising to the layman. In so far as promising is an integral part of a contract, by this definition, only a single promise is required. There must, indeed, be 'consenting wills' of at least two parties, but only as to the enforceability of a single promise, given by one party. This, I suspect, is not how most people think of a typical contract. The usual idea of a contract is that it is essentially *reciprocal* – that is, that it involves promises by both parties (if there are only two), one being given in return for the other – and that it is essentially *conditional* – in other words, each promise is an undertaking to perform some action if and only if the other party duly carries out the terms of his promise. This gap between the lay and the professional understanding of a contract is somewhat narrowed by the concept of 'consideration', which is essential to contract as understood in English law, but not, apparently, in all legal systems. According to the same authority cited above, a contractual undertaking is not valid in English law unless made in return for some valuable consideration. 'By a valuable consideration is meant something of value given or promised by one party in exchange for the promise of the other . . . Every valid contract is reducible to the form of a bargain that if I do something for you, you will do something for me' (ibid., pp.392–4). It must be noticed that this doctrine of consideration does not completely close the gap between the lay and the professional notion of contract. It makes the promising involved necessarily conditional, but not necessarily reciprocal. Suppose that A promises B to do X on condition that B does Y. If A and B agree that this promise be legally enforceable, it is a valid contract, and if B does indeed do Y then A will be required by law to do X. But this does not mean that B has necessarily made any promise, conditional or otherwise, nor that he has any contractual obligation.

But if contractual obligation, technically speaking, may be one-sided, nevertheless the model of contract employed in social contract theory is rather what I have called the lay conception, that is, of reciprocal, conditional promises and obligations. Admittedly it would be hard to claim that there is any single, rigidly defined model of the social contract – on the contrary, the concept is, as remarked above, a multifarious one, with many variations and ramifications. We must do justice to this variety, but at the same time confine our study within reasonable and manageable limits. If we were to include as social contract theories conceptions which rest political obligation on a unilateral promise the study would not only threaten to become unmanageable, but would lack coherence.

Who, then, are the parties involved in social contract theories? Broadly speaking, two models of social contract can be distinguished that differ on this score. In one, the parties are the people and their ruler or rulers – here there are just two parties, though at least one party, the people, is a collectivity. In the other, the parties are, so to speak, the building-blocks of civil society, in some cases conceived of as lesser social entities, in others as individual citizens. We thus have bilateral contracts between people and ruler, multilateral contracts between lesser social bodies, and multilateral contracts between individuals. (Rousseau's contract belongs in the third category). A particular theory of social contract can of course combine more than one of these models. In fact, we shall see as we proceed that this schematisation is too simple, but for the time being it will serve.

Having clarified the notion of contract and its relation to social contract, it will be worthwhile to look briefly at another legal analogy which has been a popular tool for analysing political authority, that of trust. Turning again to our legal authority, we find that the concept of trust belongs to the law of property. It is a case of 'duplicate ownership. Trust property is owned by two persons at the same time . . . such that one of them [the trustee] is under an obligation to use his ownership for the benefit of the other [the beneficiary]' (ibid., pp.307–8). In effect, the trustee is scarcely an owner at all, but more like an agent who must administer the property solely in the interest of the beneficiary, the purpose of this legal institution being to secure the interests of persons who for some reason cannot secure their own interests.

It is not hard to see why many thinkers have found in trust an appropriate analogy of political authority. One reason why persons may be unable to secure their interests is that they may share a common interest but be too numerous to pursue it effectively without co-ordination. It is to solve such a problem that an incorporated company, or rather its agents, are considered as trustees of the shareholders' property. Analogously, wielders of political authority may be thought of as trustees of the common interests of citizens (though not solely or necessarily of their property interests). Thus political authority can be thought of as analogous to trusteeship, and frequently has been. Indeed, many theorists have held that political authority originated in an act of entrustment by the people that charged the authorities with pursuit of the interests of citizens, and with that alone.

It is obvious that there is at least some similarity between such an entrustment, and the model of bilateral social contract between a people and their rulers (see above). Indeed, if one presses the analysis, it is hard to see any real distinction between the two. For, to entrust someone with *authority* over one, is, to all intents and purposes, to undertake (promise) to obey him so long as he uses that authority in one's interests – it is a conditional promise of obedience, similar to that supposed to be made by the people in the bilateral social contract. On the other side, it is scarcely possible to envisage an act of entrustment in which the trustee does not undertake (promise) to abide by the terms of the trust. The entrusting of authority, therefore, seems to be necessarily a contract, involving promises by both parties, at least one of these promises being conditional on due performance of his promise by the other party. The difference, if any, between this and a bilateral social contract seems vanishingly small.

Nevertheless, I shall in this book treat trust theories of political authority as separate from social contract theories (which is not to say that they can be completely ignored). This indeed is the normal practice, and is again probably necessary if the topic is to be kept manageable. Perhaps a better reason for maintaining the distinction is that – risking a broad and possibly rash generalisation – writers have used the trust analogy more to express the duties of rulers than the obligation of citizens. The element of reciprocity, crucial to contract, while implicit in this use of trust, has tended not to become explicit, and perhaps has not been noticed.

Let us now ask the question, what is the *significance*, from the standpoint of political philosophy, of the social contract theory of political authority? Really it is too early to answer this question adequately, and the variety of contract theories in any case makes it difficult to give a simple answer. Nevertheless some preliminary indications may, with due caution, be offered. Firstly, contract theory offers an account of political authority that is *voluntaristic*, that is, makes it dependent on acts of human will.[2] Legitimate authority is legitimate because those subject to it have willed to be subject to it. But, secondly, this voluntarism is also *consensual* – the theory postulates a consensus of wills among all those subject to a given legitimate authority, and this consensus is essential since we are dealing with authority exercised not over isolated individuals but over an entire society. Different contract theories express this consensualism in different ways. Some, as we have seen, treat the people as one collectivity with, in effect, a single interest and a single will, and thus able to contract with its ruler; others, more radically, postulate an agreement of the separate wills of individual citizens (there are also, as we saw above, combinations of these ideas and intermediate notions between them). Thus, thirdly, one important strand of contract theory, which may well be held to be the most important and the most typical, is a highly *individualistic* theory, grounding legitimate political authority on its acceptance by individuals. Reflection on these features at once indicates a possible strain within the theory. Is it plausible to suppose that there can be such a consensus of individual wills as to provide a viable foundation for authority? This is indeed a serious problem. The attempt at a solution leads to the fourth typical feature of social contract theory, which is *rationalism*. If the individual wills are not wilful but rational, it is postulated, consensus can be reached. None the less, there remains a tension within social contract theory between its voluntarism, which in principle respects people's choices, whatever they may be, and its rationalism, which supposes that their choices must follow very definite lines.

These various features of social contract theory can be thrown into sharper relief by a brief look at various other, non-contractual ways of understanding political authority, especially those available to theorists in the earlier phases of European political thought. (Needless to say, theoretical ingenuity has produced numerous composite systems combining these alternative understandings with contractarian ideas and with each other, more or less coherently. This, however, does not alter the fact that they *are* alternatives to contract, which we can better understand by contrast with these rivals, considered in, so to speak, a pure form). We can first of all divide the alternatives into two classes, naturalistic and supernaturalistic.

By supernaturalistic conceptions I mean simply those that base legitimate political authority on the will of God. Such a theory is voluntaristic in a formal sense, but the will in question is not a human but a divine will. A typical example of this style of thinking is the theory of the divine right of kings. However, knowledge of the divine will is difficult and disputable to say the least, and so many different and incompatible theories can be derived from that premise. According to the great German historian of ideas, Otto Gierke, the characteristic medieval inference from the primacy of God's will was not divine kingship but the unity of Christendom under Pope and Emperor (GMA, 7f.). As Gierke points out, this was a holistic conception, in which the individual and lesser social and political units were subordinated to the whole, Christendom. Thus theistic political thought might be holistic or monarchical, but if God is concerned with the salvation of the ordinary person it might just as well give rise to populist or individualist ideas. It could be held that the voice of the people is the voice of God. It could, and did (as we shall see at some length) give rise to social contract theories.

Naturalistic political theory contrasts both with supernaturalistic and with contract theory (though again surprising combinations are possible). Briefly, on this view, political life including authority is a natural growth which neither depends on nor calls for any self-conscious acts of human will. The most important and influential example of this attitude is Aristotelian theory, so pervasive in the later Middle Ages. According to Aristotle, man is by nature a political animal – *zoon politikon*. Men and women naturally came together to form households, households naturally amalgamated into villages, and several villages, finally, into a 'city' or 'state' (Aristotle, *Politics*, book I, chapters 1 and 2). Aristotle's theory is teleological and therefore holistic; the entire evolution is governed by its end, and hence the final and most inclusive association – the state – has priority over individuals and lesser associations. (As a matter of fact the medieval conception described by Gierke has much of Aristotelianism in it, but with the addition of a more inclusive supreme political unit and the substitution of God's will for nature). For Aristotle, each level of human association has its own function – that of the state is realisation of the good life. Hence, when Aristotle discusses various different forms of political organisation he is concerned to assess them purely from this point of view, and not in the least in terms of any contract. Nevertheless, we shall see that medieval and later political thought was quite capable of combining Aristotelian naturalism with contractarianism.

Another form of naturalism that is worth mentioning is patriarchalism. Unlike the other modes of thought considered so far, this is always a defence of a particular political system, monarchy, and usually, indeed, absolute monarchy. For this theory, the model for understanding political authority is the family, assumed to be ruled monarchically by the father. Aristotle, like the patriarchalists, had considered monarchy to be natural within the family or household, but unlike them he drew a sharp distinction between family/

household and state. To the patriarchalists, just as children are naturally subject to the father who begot them, so private citizens are naturally subject to the father of their country, their king. Not, of course, that he is literally their father – rather, he is the inheritor of the natural authority of fathers. According to Sir Robert Filmer, author of *Patriarcha*, this authority originally inhered in Adam, the father of the human race, and passed by biological – that is, natural – descent to his heirs. As the race increased in numbers, so too did families, turning thereby into kingdoms, but the basis of authority did not alter (F, 11–13). This version of patriarchalism is also a version of supernaturalism in that it is ultimately based on the will of God. From the point of view of social contract theory, its main significance is as an important rival to the latter at the period of its highest development. Contract theorists devoted a good deal of their attention to the relation between the family and civil society, and to giving an alternative account to the patriarchalist one.

It is now time to give the reader a brief overview of the plan of this book. Social contract theory can be considered in two ways, historically and analytically. Both approaches will be adopted here. Historically, contract theory has known two periods of flourishing, one lasting from the sixteenth to the eighteenth century, the other the contemporary revival. Though there is a clear continuity between the theories of the two periods, they are nevertheless sufficiently different to demand separate treatment. Analytically, there are problems and issues that seem to pertain to social contract theory as such, and others that pertain more particularly to one or other period of its history. These will be discussed at appropriate points in the book – the aim is to alternate, and integrate, history and analysis in as coherent a fashion as possible.

The next section of the book will take up the historical exposition of the first great period of contract theory. Actually, we shall begin before that period, with the medieval centuries, because it is only in the light of that pre-history that the ideas of the later period can be properly understood. Some, indeed, might object that it is necessary to begin even further back, with classical and especially Greek political thought. I have decided, however, not to adopt this plan. On the whole, Greek contractarian thought has survived in too fragmentary or dubious a form to make a satisfactory topic in its own right, and it is too remote in time to be easily integrated into the later story. On the other hand, it would be foolish to deny the importance of the classical influence on this, as on almost every other aspect of western culture. It seems best, however, to recognise this, as it were, retrospectively, when dealing with later thinkers.

I mentioned above the need to integrate history and analysis. This means that, though the next section of the book is historical, it will be to some extent structured by analytic concerns. It seems to me essential to give the narrative a focus, so that it does not appear a mere inconsequent succession of loosely related ideas. To provide such a focus I shall select the greatest masterpiece of contractarian philosophy, perhaps of all political philosophy (its only rival is Plato's *Republic*) – namely, the *Leviathan* of Thomas Hobbes, published in 1651. Some might consider this an inappropriate choice, for the *Leviathan* is often held to be untypical of contractarian thought in general. This is true in some respects, notably in the ideological use that Hobbes makes of the contract. In respect of the general *structure* of the theory, however, it is absolutely characteristic, and it displays this structure, which is, in a way, the logical culmination of all earlier contractarian thought, with classic clarity. I shall therefore use this Hobbesian structure as a framework for the first part of the history of social contract theory.

The elements of the Hobbesian theory are, briefly, these. Men are exhibited in what has come to be called the *state of nature* (Hobbes himself in the *Leviathan* calls it the estate of nature, or the natural condition of mankind). This is a definition of what men and their relations are *naturally* like, that is, in the absence of any deliberately contrived institutions. Contrary to the Aristotelian view, it is a non-political condition, devoid of any political authority. In it all men have a *natural right* of liberty, but it is none the less a patently unsatisfactory state of affairs, and reason clearly demonstrates the preferability of political society under an effective authority. This must therefore be established by general agreement, by what Hobbes calls a covenant of every man with every man, or, in other words, a *social contract*. This contract is, then, the basis of legitimate political authority and of political obligation. In making it and abiding by it, Hobbes says, men obey the law of nature, the true moral law. Hobbes' theory thus combines with the idea of social contract the ideas of state of nature, natural right, and law of nature. In our examination of the development of contract theory we shall be on the lookout for these ideas also.

2   The Middle Ages and the Renaissance

'No man can make himself king or emperor, the people raise a man above them in this way in order that he may govern them in accordance with right reason, give to each one his own, protect the good, destroy the wicked, and administer justice to every man. But if he violates the contract (*pactum*) under which he was elected, disturbing and confounding that which he was established to set in order, then the people is justly and reasonably released from its obligation to obey him. For he was the first to break the faith that bound them together.'

If, the writer goes on, a ruler acts like a tyrant, destroying peace and justice, then the people, absolved thereby from its oath of allegiance, is free to depose him and set up another.

The writer cited above is Manegold of Lautenbach in Alsace, addressing himself to issues of political obligation around the year 1080.[1] His significance for this study is that he does so in terms of a contract. Manegold, apparently, was the first man (or the first since ancient times) to offer a general contractual theory of political authority. The word 'theory' is important: for Manegold is not alluding to any particular contract, but is rather claiming that a contract is the inherent foundation of every people's relation to its ruler, setting the conditions and limits of the latter's authority and the former's obligation. Nor was Manegold's use of the contract idea casual or accidental, for in another passage he drew a famous comparison between this contract of rulership and an everyday contract of employment. 'If a man has hired a swineherd to look after his pigs in return for a proper wage, and he, instead of looking after them, steals them or kills them or loses them, will not that man not only refuse to pay him the wage, but also dismiss

12

him?' (CIII, 166–7). Just as the rights and tenure of the swineherd depend on his contract of employment, so do those of the ruler depend on the contract of rulership – indeed all the more so, just because (as Manegold hastens to add) the task of a ruler is so much more important and exalted than a swineherd's.

In spite of that last addition, it is clear that the aim of Manegold's remarks is to deflate the pretensions, often quasi-divine, of kings and emperors – even although Manegold fully accepts that secular authority is a part of the divine order. They thus mark the initiation of a characteristic use of contract theory. But we cannot come close to grasping Manegold's real meaning without some appreciation of the historical context; namely, the endemic medieval struggle of Emperor and Pope, and more particularly the famous investiture controversy between Pope Gregory VII and the Emperor Henry IV, in which each attempted to depose the other.[2] In this light, Manegold's theory of political authority is revealed as less populist and also less contractualist than appears at first sight. Manegold was a papalist partisan, who wrote to undermine the claims of *secular* authority only. Gregory's attempted deposition of Henry took the form of excommunication, a declaration absolving his feudal vassals from their oaths of allegiance, and support for a rival claimant to the imperial throne. The pope, in fact, took advantage of the circumstance that he was not the only person wishing to see Henry deposed – so too did an important element among the German princes, who had been in revolt against him for some years before his excommunication. The conclusion, therefore, of Manegold's theory is that the pope is entitled to depose a ruler (in particular an emperor) who breaks the contract with his people which conferred authority on him. Manegold allots to the pope the quasi-judicial function of enforcing this contract.

A number of comments on Manegold's contract theory are in order. First, it is a contract theory of *secular* authority only – not of political authority as such. It is clear that Manegold (in line with medieval theory generally) saw political authority as divided between the two powers, spiritual and temporal, and it is only the latter that he sees as contractually based. The political authority of the spiritual power – the papacy – is derived by apostolic succession from the authority vested by God in St Peter. Second, there was no logical necessity that Manegold should use a contractualist argument in support of his general position, namely the exaltation of the political authority of the Pope in relation to the Emperor. He might have reached the same conclusion more directly, as a deduction from God's will – many papalist writers did just that.[3] The form of Manegold's argument undoubtedly owes much to the circumstance that the Pope's enemy happened to be at the same time in conflict with an important element among his 'people'. This illustrates a general feature of social contract theory – a certain looseness of logical fit between the theory and its ideological use, which, as we shall see, gives it considerable versatility as a partisan weapon. Third, it is noteworthy that the contract theory of political authority here makes its debut as part of a dispute about the religious powers of secular rulers. Manegold, indeed, accused Henry IV of forcing his subjects into apostasy and idolatry (meaning thereby, disobedience to the papacy), implying that this too was in breach of his contract (CIII, 164–5). This religious element has quite detailed parallels in important later developments of contract theory, and shows us that the theory, like so much of the whole of European political history, was crucially influenced by the division between church and state.

Although Manegold's contract theory is not a complete theory of political authority and was not strictly necessary to his general position, it is nevertheless of the greatest significance. It is therefore important to ask why it should have occurred to him. In other words, what elements in European political experience and theory might have made it seem to him an appropriate form of argument? Commentators have pointed to a number of likely sources for the development of contract theory. One is the inheritance of Roman law, in which the concept of contract was well developed. Another important Roman law concept which has been cited is the *lex regia*, according to which the Roman Emperors – of whom the medieval Emperor was held to be the successor – owed their authority to a grant from the people, in whom that authority originally inhered. However, this cannot have much relevance to Manegold's theory, for the general recovery of Roman law by medieval jurists dates only from the twelfth century (GMA, 39), and in any case a grant of authority is not a contract, or at least not a contract in the sense of social contract theory, namely one which is (as explained above) conditional and reciprocal. On the other hand, a model for such a contract can be found in another source – the Bible. 'So all the elders of Israel came to the King to Hebron; and King David made a covenant with them in Hebron before the Lord; and they anointed David King over Israel.'[4] David's kingship, in other words, depended on a contract made with the elders as representatives of the people of Israel. One might expect passages such as these to be very familiar to Manegold; nevertheless (unlike later contract theorists) he does not use them explicitly.

Thus, while the legacy of Roman law and Judeo-Christianity were later to be of great importance, the key influences on Manegold's contractarian thought are to be sought elsewhere – in the political practice of medieval Europe, and especially in two closely related elements of that practice, feudalism and medieval monarchy. The importance of feudalism can scarcely be over-emphasised. For feudalism was precisely a system of legal contracts between superiors and inferiors – between lord and vassal. In this relation both parties had contractual rights and obligations. On the one hand the vassal was bound to offer his lord certain services and support him as required; on the other, the lord must protect his vassals and administer justice to them – clearly political functions offering an obvious parallel to those of the ruler. And the ruler – the king – was in fact a part of this system, as the highest feudal lord in his realm. In a society thoroughly feudalised, every single person would be party to a contract of a quasi-political kind, not usually directly with the ruler, but with a feudal superior linked in his turn, directly or indirectly, with further superiors in an ascending series culminating always in the ruler himself. Since the king was a feudal lord, he, like his subjects, was bound by feudal contracts. Furthermore, feudal law developed a remedy for breach of contract by a feudal superior, the *diffidatio* (Ullman, 1967, p.64): by this means a vassal could in such a case repudiate his own contractual obligations to his lord. Various European feudal law books set out in detail the procedures by which a vassal might seek redress in the event of breach of faith by his lord – not excluding the king.[5]

Marc Bloch, the great historian of feudalism, remarked that such ideas were bound to be transferred to the political sphere proper (Bloch, 1965, p.451). The theory of Manegold of Lautenbach is just such a transfer. Indeed, his claim that the Emperor, Henry IV, had broken the contract with his people by which every secular ruler is bound, was for Manegold a premise that allowed him to draw the conclusion that for this reason his enemies among the German princes, who were among his chief vassals, were absolved from their oath of allegiance to him – just as if Henry had broken a feudal contract. If, says Manegold, the ruler acts tyrannically, and destroys peace and justice, any man who has sworn allegiance to him is absolved, and the people is free to depose him. This juxtaposition makes as clear as it could be the parallel in Manegold's mind between his contract theory and the obligations of feudalism. Indeed, Manegold subsequently appears to identify 'the people', who are entitled to depose their ruler, with the princes collectively (CIII, 164–5).

Yet feudalism cannot be the whole story. Feudalism is indeed a system of contracts, but the contract between a feudal lord and his vassal formalises and regulates a *pre-existing* relationship of inequality. The superiority of the lord is not *created* by the feudal contract. It is not imaginable that, had the parties involved so decided, the roles of lord and vassal might have been reversed, as would be the case if the contract were a contract between equals. Yet Manegold's insistence that 'no man can make himself king or emperor', that kingship depends on the decision of 'the people' (that is, their leaders, the princes), still more his comparison of kingship with a contract of employment, imply that the superiority of the ruler *does* depend on the contract, but for which he would not be superior to his fellow-contractors. This is a crucial aspect of contract theory, and to explain its appearance in Manegold's thought we must look beyond feudalism.

The development of the feudal system in Europe dates from the collapse of the Carolingian empire of the ninth century; but, even before this, Europe knew political institutions of a contractual or quasi-contractual kind. The Germanic peoples who invaded and destroyed the western Roman Empire eventually established territorial kingdoms, but these kings were far from absolute.[6] In the first place, they were normally elective, at least in the sense that the succession of a new king had to be approved by the leading men of the kingdom. There was no automatic rule of primogeniture or anything else. Secondly, it was understood that the king would rule in accordance with the laws and customs of the kingdom, an understanding that was normally given expression in the king's coronation oath and, abnormally, reiterated at times of political crisis. Taken together, these two facts – that the king was elected, and that on the occasion of his election he explicitly recognised that his actions were constrained by law and custom – come close to constituting a political contract, to the effect that his recognition as king was *conditional* on his promise to respect the laws and customs. Indeed, there is more than one such case where the concept of a contract (*pactum*) was made explicit, the earliest apparently occurring in the kingdom of the Visigoths in 633 (Gough, 1957, p. 24). It is noteworthy that the election of the king or approval of his succession by the leading men of the kingdom was construed as the act of the people as a whole. This immemorial understanding no doubt made it natural for Manegold of Lautenbach, as we have seen, to interpret the feudal contract between the Emperor and the German princes as a contract between ruler and people, and to build on to these actual, particular, and quasi-legal or constitutional relationships a general theory of political contract.

What became of that theory after Manegold? According to the medieval historian Walter Ullmann, the idea that there is a contract between ruler and people remained a minority view among political theorists. Nevertheless, it did not die out. For example, the twelfth century canonist and (again) upholder of papal authority, Rufinus, reiterated Manegold's argument: 'When the king is instituted, he enters into a tacit contract (*pactio quaedam tacita*) with the people, with a view to ruling the people in a humane manner.'[7] Again, Manegold's view is preserved in such a leading authority as St Thomas Aquinas, who, in the middle of the thirteenth century, wrote (in *De Regimine Principum*), that the people may deprive a tyrannical ruler of his authority since 'he has deserved that the contract (*pactum*) with him not be kept by his subjects' (Barker, 1947, pp.vii–viii). Clearly, a contractual relationship between peoples and their secular rulers remained a part of the conceptual stock-in-trade of medieval thinkers. However, the remarks of Rufinus and St Thomas cited above do not add anything new to the ideas of Manegold. The next original contribution to the theory appears to have been made only in the fourteenth century.

The original contract

By the early fourteenth century, the European political landscape had changed considerably since the days of Manegold, but not out of all recognition. The papacy and the empire were still at loggerheads, and once against their rivalry was complicated by the claims and ambitions of third parties. By now, however, the latter were not feudal vassals of the emperor, but kings of nascent nation-states asserting their independence of him, and in particular the king of France. Of the three main parties in this power struggle, the weakest was the Empire which, to some contemporaries, even appeared, after the assassination of the Emperor Albert of Austria in 1308, to be on the verge of extinction (Fowler, 1967, p.166).

As in previous (and later) centuries, political struggles called forth works of political theory that combined in varying proportions partisan propaganda and philosophical objectivity. One of these works is significant in the history of contract theory. Its author was Engelbert of Volkersdorf, abbot of the important Austrian monastery of Admont. Engelbert's view of government is a synthesis (probably derived from St. Thomas Aquinas) of super-naturalist, Aristotelian and contractualist elements. For him, as for all medieval Christian thinkers, the ultimate ground of political authority is the will of God. He holds also, in Aristotelian fashion, that political organisation, and hence the subordination of some men to to others, is natural to mankind, and serves a specific function – the attainment of peace and justice. Yet although natural, the authority of states *originates* in a particular act of will, a contract of subjection, *pactum subiectionis*, which men entered into 'in order to be ruled, protected and preserved' (ibid., pp.167–70). Where Manegold's contract of rulership was a generalisation of the oaths and promises exchanged by feudal kings and their subjects, the contract of which Engelbert speaks relates to the first foundation of political authority. He is thus the begetter of an idea destined to have a long and important career – what was later called 'the original contract'.

Despite this innovation, the implications of the contract for Engelbert appear similar to what they had been for Manegold. A free people is entitled to choose its ruler; a ruler who abuses his authority becomes a tyrant, and should be deposed. Yet this appearance of similarity is deceptive for, unlike Manegold, Engelbert wrote to uphold the authority of the Empire, then (c.1310) at such a low ebb, but considered by Engelbert to be essential to the peace and safety of Christendom (Lewis, 1974, p.444). His remarks about the deposition of tyrants, in which he agrees with Manegold, are of theoretical significance only; for practical purposes, what is of prime importance to him is the potential benefits of secular authority, and of the Empire in particular. This contrast between the first two major contract theorists illustrates an important general characteristic of contract theory, its double-edged quality. It can be used either to uphold political authority, or to restrain and limit it. For one does not (freely) make a contract unless one expects some benefit thereby; at the same time contracting with a partner is designed to constrain the latter's behaviour. According as one or other aspect is emphasised, a contractual view of political authority can either stress the advantages of that authority, or its dangers which must be controlled.

Engelbert's blend of contractualism and Aristotelianism is a little uneasy. A universal Empire, he argues, is preferable to a series of independent kingdoms, because the 'invention and establishment of kingdoms and kings in human society comes from art and reason', and 'art and reason imitate nature'. But nature, Engelbert thinks, established the first kingdoms as universal monarchies, among the brute creation – 'among beasts, the lion is king of all, and among birds, the eagle is king.' Hence men too should have only one king and lord (ibid., pp.473–4). Apart from the quaint zoology of this, it is questionable whether a human 'art and reason' which must simply imitate 'nature' in such a simple way is playing any real theoretical role. By and large, Engelbert's more persuasive arguments for the Empire are not contractarian but functional and, one might say, Aristotelian – a great kingdom, on balance, would be more likely to achieve the ends of political organisation (justice, security, felicity or the good life) than a series of small ones (ibid., pp.445–6). In view of all this one may wonder why Engelbert chose to introduce the original contract into his theory at all.

At least a partial answer to this question is possible. It is natural enough that writers such as Engelbert, who wished to stress the benefits of secular political authority, should make a comparison between life under such an authority and life without it, or before it. From this it is only a step to a concern with the origins of that authority, and the reasons why it was established. That such notions were current at the time when Engelbert was writing is shown by the work of a famous contemporary and, in a sense,

enemy of Engelbert, namely John of Paris. In the power struggles
of the day John was the foremost theoretical champion of the
claims of the King of France to complete political independence
from both the Empire and the papacy. John, unlike Engelbert,
did not make theoretical use of the idea of a contract; but like
him he concerned himself with the origin of government, which
he held to be the result of persuasion by the most rational men
of their fellows.[8] Somewhat earlier, the French feudal lawyer
Beaumanoir had depicted the people as first choosing kings in
order to end a previous state of war among them (ibid., pp.343–
4). Engelbert's *pactum* fits into this general picture.

That picture broaches a theme highly significant for the development of contract theory – the state of men without, or before
government, which would later come to be known as the 'state of
nature.' It could not be so described, however, so long as thinkers
held, like Engelbert, to Aristotelian ideas, according to which
man's natural condition is political. But regardless of the name
given to it, an account of the pre-political state was bound to
become an integral part of a contract theory which was a theory
of the origin of government. We shall therefore turn now to the
history of this idea.

Pre-political man

Speculation on pre-political man and the transition to the political
state goes back to classical Greece, and more particularly, it seems,
to the sophists of the fifth century BC, whose individualistic point
of view would naturally lead them to see the existence of political
communities as needing explanation. For Protagoras, the greatest
of the sophists, the origin of 'cities' is part of a theory of progress,
in particular moral progress. At first, he held, men lived 'scattered',
in a state of self-destructive mutual hostility. Escape from this
condition required that they master the 'political art', for which
certain virtues were necessary, such as a sense of justice (said by
Protagoras – perhaps not seriously – to have been brought to man
by divine intervention). The laws of the state (*nomoi*) are necessary
restraints (Guthrie, 1969, pp.63–6).

Interestingly, a number of Protagoras's sophist contemporaries
conceived of these laws as the terms of contracts between previously

unrestrained individuals, a fact which has led some commentators to see these writers as the originators of social contract theory (ibid., chapter V, esp. pp.141–7). In my opinion this is a misinterpretation, at least if a social contract theory is defined as a theory in which the justification and/or proper limits of political authority are derived from a contract. None of the alleged sophist contract theorists do this. The reason is that they use in a particular way the Greek distinction between nature (*physis*) and law or convention (*nomos*).[9] Law, which is the outcome of contracts, is in their view merely conventional, not natural, and hence of comparatively little worth. According to the famous argument reported by Glaucon in Plato's *Republic* (in order to be refuted by Socrates), it is natural for men to inflict injustice on one another whenever they can; laws are 'contracts of mutual abstention from injustice' that men have entered into in order to avoid suffering the injustice of others, but evade wherever possible. Abiding by these 'laws and covenants' out of a sense of justice is thus a recipe for suffering endless misery, and is nothing but folly.[10] An alternative view is that of the sophist Hippias, who upheld the 'unwritten laws' considered binding in every country, as against the positive laws which are merely 'covenants made by the citizens' of particular states (ibid., pp.118–19,138). On both of these views, the laws of states are unworthy of much respect because they conflict with 'nature', whether that nature is identified with the pursuit of self-interest or with a universal morality superior to local and transient conventions. For Protagoras, on the other hand, the laws should be respected, but they are not contractual. None of these theories adopt the major premise of contract theory – that one is bound by one's contract.[11] The relevance to contract theory of theories such as that of Protagoras and that reported by Glaucon is, rather, that they manifest a concern with the origin of political institutions and the reasons for that origin.

Many centuries were to pass before that concern gave birth, with Engelbert of Volkersdorf, to the theory of the original contract. We cannot here follow the history of this lengthy gestation, but one writer who deserves mention because of his importance as a transmitter of Greek thought to the later European tradition is the Roman lawyer Cicero. In his *De Inventione* and *Pro Sestio*, Cicero presents a picture of human evolution not dissimilar to that of Protagoras, in which a primitive pre-political stage, marked by dispersed wandering 'like animals', fighting, and a low level of civilisation, gives way to political society, respect for law, and a more civilised life.[12] In Cicero, however, the agency of this change is not the gods, but the eloquence of wise men – a view which, as we saw above, was still adopted in the fourteenth century by John of Paris.

Despite the impression given by many of the most authoritative commentators,[13] neither Protagoras nor Cicero conceived of the primitive pre-political condition of men as a state of nature. No more than Aristotle, it seems, could these theorists of human progress see man's uncivilised, pre-political condition as his natural state. The roots of this notion, I believe, have to be sought in another tradition of thought, also ancient, which may be called the Stoic-Christian tradition, and which viewed human history not as progress but as decline.

In our brief discussion above of some sophistic thought, we noted two contrasting views of 'nature' in relation to human conduct – respectively, that it licenses unrestrained egoism, and that it prescribes universally binding moral norms. This fundamental duality was to continue for many centuries, and is of the greatest importance for social contract theory. One reason for this is the close connection between that theory and the concept of natural law. That concept is already almost explicit in Hippias's contrast between mere contractual law which is not natural, and an unwritten universal law (which presumably is). It is definitely explicit in Aristotle, though rather peripheral to his thought; while the Stoic school made it a central element of their moral and political theory (ibid., pp.118,123–4). With Stoic thought in general, it spread from Greece to Rome, and it is to the Roman Stoic writer, Seneca, that we must now turn. Seneca combined the Stoic conception of nature with the ancient Greek notion of the succession of the Ages. The first men, he held, lived in the Golden Age, and 'being still uncorrupted, followed nature' (Lovejoy and Boas, 1965, p.269). Seneca, in other words, has a conception of the natural state of man, or the 'state of nature'; and 'nature' is to him a standard of moral excellence, so that the natural state is also a Golden Age. But although this state is primitive, it is not (contrary to the standard interpretation)[14] pre-political: rather, 'rulership was confided to the wise', for 'it is the way of nature to make the inferior subject to the superior'. Alas, such a happy state of affairs did not last: mankind was to decline from the Golden Age. 'When vices crept in and these kingships were converted into tyrannies, the need of laws began to be felt'. Seneca, then, gives us a state of nature, but it does not yet have any negative features that explain the need for, or the origin of, government.

The diffusion to Rome of Stoic ideas about nature did not stop at pagan writers such as Seneca; it exerted a major influence also on the Christian Fathers. Thus Augustine of Hippo, greatest of the Latin Fathers, conceived of a state of nature not unlike that of Seneca before him. According to Augustine, the first human beings were 'just men' who lived according to the 'order of nature' in which God originally created mankind.[15] What is more, this primitive, natural and godly state was (unlike Seneca's Golden Age) pre-political. 'God did not wish the rational being, made in his own image, to have dominion over any but irrational creatures, not man over man, but man over the beasts. Hence the first just men were set up as shepherds of flocks, rather than as kings of men'. Implicit in this passage, and explicit in other writings of the Fathers,[16] is the notion of the natural equality and freedom of all men, made in God's image – a freedom and equality once actual in the state of nature.

The Augustinian pre-political state of nature still does not suffer from any inherent defects that might explain the need for government or its origin. Rather, on the Patristic view, these defects arose later as a result of the Fall of Man. Already in the second century this was clearly stated by St Irenaeus: because men disobeyed God and hated their fellows, falling into confusion and disorder, God established the authority of man over man, in order to compel some degree of justice and righteousness.[17] In brief, government has been divinely instituted as a partial remedy for human sinfulness. This theory of the origin of government is of course not a contractual one; but it is of interest in relation to contract theory in that it complicates the Stoic-derived conception of the natural state of man. After all, fallen man's sinfulness, according to Christian dogma, is now an inherent part of his nature (hence the need for salvation by the grace of God). In a certain sense, the confusion and disorder into which men fell through disobedience must therefore be their natural state. There is here a foreshadowing of the later contractarian conception of the state of nature, as a pre-political condition subject to defects for which government is the remedy.

In the Patristic writings the mingling of Christian ideas and Stoic philosophy thus produces an ambivalent or dualistic conception of nature somewhat reminiscent of that already seen in the Greek sophists. A rather similar process can be traced in another highly influential body of thought, Roman law. One of the most notable ideas developed by the Roman imperial jurists was that of the natural law, *ius naturale* – clearly a Stoic inheritance, probably transmitted through the writings of Cicero. 'There is a true law, namely right reason', wrote Cicero, 'which is in accordance with nature, applies to all men, and is unchangeable and eternal' (Sabine, 1963, p.164). The same view was taken by the jurists whose opinions were collected in the sixth century in the *Digests* and the *Institutes*, and they placed this natural law of reason above the civil law of states (*ius civile*). Like the Christian Fathers they held that all men are by nature (that is, by the law of nature rather than in the state of nature) free and equal (ibid., pp.167–9). With the revival of Roman law in the later middle ages, the agreement on natural human freedom and equality of two such authoritative traditions of thought led to a widespread acceptance that government originated by consent of the governed, and even, in agreement with Engelbert of Volkersdorf, by a compact of subjection.

It was not, however, Engelbert or Manegold who was the chief authority in the later medieval centuries for the concept of a contract of rulership, but rather the great St Augustine himself. In a passage of his *Confessions* asserting the absolute necessity of obedience to God, Augustine compared this obligation with the obligation of obedience to temporal authority, which, he remarks, is based on a general contract of human society to obey their kings (*generale pactum societatis humanae oboedire Regibus suis*). This passing remark of Augustine was incorporated in Gratian's *Decretum*, the great twelfth century compilation of canon law, and thus passed on to later thinkers (D'Addio, 1954, p.189). In this way it provided an alternative source, in addition to the feudal notions that inspired Manegold, for the concept of a contract between ruler and people, and in some cases an original contract. Engelbert himself did not cite this passage of Augustine as an authority; but later thinkers not infrequently did so.[18] At least one writer, the late fifteenth-century Neapolitan jurist Paride del Pozzo, used

Augustine's formula to argue that the people are obliged to obey their King only if he governs within the law of nature and of nations (*ius naturale et gentium*), otherwise he has broken his contract and may be deposed and even killed (ibid., pp.385–7).

Salamonio

Paride, writing at the end of the Middle Ages, exhibits the dual intellectual heritage of Christianity and Roman law. The same is true of another group of writers, the humanist jurists of the Renaissance, to whom we must now turn our attention. They too inherited in their turn the Roman law concept of the *ius naturale*. But for Renaissance humanism, no writer had greater authority than Cicero; hence among these jurists there was general acceptance of the Ciceronian picture of the barbaric, animal-like pre-political stage of man's history (Tuck, 1979, pp.33–7). In the light of the Christian conception of man's sinful nature, this phase could now be seen as natural, and, therefore, governed by natural law. But such a natural law could not be the supreme and universal moral law of the Stoics and of medieval orthodoxy; rather this *ius naturale* was the law taught by nature to all animals, and to men only in so far as they too were animal-like.[19] It dictated certain 'normal' modes of behaviour, morally acceptable because sanctioned by nature, but morally inferior to strictly human law – the *ius gentium* – and the civil law.

It was out of this background of ideas that arose, in the early sixteenth century, a major development of social contract theory: the *De Principatu* of Mario Salamonio of Rome, written in the years 1511–13.[20] Salamonio was one of the most distinguished jurists of his day, and – whereas the contract theory of Manegold, for example, was derived from concepts of feudalism and pre-feudal monarchy – Salamonio's is a contract theory based on concepts of Roman law. The political context of his argument, too, was inevitably different from that of Manegold or Engelbert. No longer was the proper role of Pope and Emperor the dominant issue of European politics. In Italy's patchwork of small city-states, the main struggle was between the forces of republicanism and despotic monarchy. It is true that, in Salamonio's native city of Rome, the power of the Pope was still at issue – but here he figured as temporal, not merely spiritual, ruler. 1511, the year when Salamonio began to write his *De Principatu*, was also the year of a rising against the Pope's temporal power in the city, coupled with demands for a restoration of its ancient republican liberties; and the *De Principatu* is an expression of Salamonio's support for the insurrectionist cause. If Manegold's is a papalist contractarianism, and Engelbert's an imperialist contractarianism, the theory of Salamonio is a republican contractarianism.

Salamonio's republican sympathies did not lead him to deny the legitimacy of all princely authority. Rather, he maintained that princes are no more than chief magistrates, bound by the laws like all citizens of the republic. They are not *legibus solutus* – above the law (S, 11f.). For princes, says Salamonio, did not always exist. Nature and God created all men equal at first; later, however, men found it urgently necessary to erect kingdoms and princedoms. Salamonio stresses that the latter arose 'by agreements of men', and interprets this, by now, familiar idea in terms of the ancient Roman law concept of the *lex regia*, by which, it was held, the people first delegated authority to a prince (S, 16f.). But Salamonio goes further than this. A state, or *civitas*, is, according to him, a civil partnership – *civilis societas*. This is a most pregnant term which we would now naturally translate as 'civil society'; but in Roman law *societas* is a partnership, implying free contractual agreement of the partners. Salamonio applies just this concept to the state – it is a civil partnership constituted by the free contract of citizens, and the terms of their contract are the laws of the state without which the state cannot exist (S, 28–9). The prince, like all citizens, is thus bound by the laws; it is even permissible to kill, as a tyrant, a law-breaking ruler.[21]

In a certain sense Salamonio's contractualism brings us back full circle to the ideas of some of the Greek sophists, discussed above, who likewise saw the laws as contracts or covenants between citizens. But there is also a huge difference between the sophists and Salamonio. For the sophists, the contractual origin of laws shows their transitoriness and lack of real obligatory force; for Salamonio, it is just their contractual origin that makes them binding. Between the sophists and Salamonio there has risen to general acceptance the premise needed to turn the sophist ideas into a general contract theory; the premise of a moral obligation to keep promises. Salamonio, again unlike the sophists, did not contrast convention unfavourably with nature, which for him had come to have, at best, a limited or ambiguous legitimacy. The obligation to keep promises, like all moral obligations, is a matter not of the *ius naturale*, but of the *ius gentium*.[22] This principle of human moral law is the foundation of his contract theory.

Many commentators have pointed out the originality of Salamonio's contractarianism.[23] For the first time the parties to the contract are not people and ruler, but individual citizens – law, says Salamonio, is a contract (*pactio*) *inter cives*, comparable to a 'contract made in a business partnership' – a strikingly individualistic analogy. Indeed, says Salamonio, a people (*populus*) is not really a single person, but is considered so only by fiction; in reality it is 'nothing but a certain multitude of men' (S, 27,29). To be sure, he is much concerned with the relation between people and ruler, but this is determined by a law (the *lex regia*) which like law in general must presumably be determined by prior agreement among citizens. The prince is bound by it, not only because it sets the terms of princely authority, but also because he too is a citizen and thus a party to the contract *inter cives* by which it was instituted. Thus the natural freedom and equality of men are reconciled with political authority.

However, Salamonio, unlike later theorists, did not portray his contract as the act of individuals endowed with prior natural rights – nature, as we saw, was not for Salamonio a source of moral rights and obligations. Indeed, nature for him seems to have had mainly negative connotations: 'by nature', he remarks, men were made naked, poor, unable to provide for their needs without mutual aid – hence the origin of states (S, 42). Despite Salamonio's frequent and respectful allusions to Aristotle, this is a profoundly un-Aristotelian concept, prefiguring – despite the absence of natural rights – the later elaboration of the state of nature as an integral part of contract theory.

3 The Reformation and the Wars of Religion

The *De Principatu* of Salamonio was written just before the outbreak of the cataclysm that shattered the unity of Western Europe – the Reformation. As we shall see, it was this event that led to the heyday of contractarian political thought, stemming in the first instance from the efforts of radical Protestants to justify their political stance, and later from the attempted refutations of their opponents. So widespread does the use of contractarian concepts become in this period that it will not be possible to follow all their ramifications. Only the major contributors to contract theory can be considered, and thinkers, however important in other respects – for example, Hooker or Grotius – whose allusions to contract are merely tangential, or unspecific, or simply unoriginal, will perforce be ignored, or at best briefly mentioned. Such selectivity, however regrettable, is unavoidable.

Before we turn to developments after the Reformation, it will be appropriate, in the light of what we have learnt about the earlier theorists, to consider a way of distinguishing types of contract theory (or of contracts postulated by theorists) that has been popular with scholars, and stems initially from the work of the great Otto Gierke. Gierke distinguished between the contract of rulership, or *Herrschaftsvertrag*, and the social contract, *Gesellschaftsvertrag* (GPT, part two, chapter 2; GNL, 106). By the former, Gierke referred to the agreement between people and ruler which, according to such theorists as Manegold and Engelbert, legitimised the ruler's authority; by the social contract he meant the idea that the state or civil society is the outcome of an agreement among pre-political individuals (or among lesser associations themselves formed by individual agreements). In its essentials Gierke's distinction was maintained by two leading

English students of contract theory, J. W. Gough and Sir Ernest Barker, with slight changes of terminology (or retranslation); they spoke of the contract of government, and the contract of society, or social contract proper (Gough, 1957, pp.2–3; Barker, 1947, pp.xii–xiii). In these terms Gough claimed Salamonio as the first writer to give a clear account of the contract of society (Gough, 1957, p.47), and with considerable justice.

However, these distinctions and terminology are not completely satisfactory. The term *social* (as distinct from governmental) contract, gives the misleading impression that that contract is not a political matter, and raises the question, what its relevance could be to political obligation. In fact, the so-called social contract (proper), or contract of society, *is* a political matter, for it is an agreement (as we saw with Salamonio) on the laws by which the society is to be governed. But the relevance of this contract to political obligation is somewhat indirect: in itself it creates only an obligation to obey the agreed laws. However, these laws constrain subsequently constituted political authority, whether this subsequent constitution results from an act of delegation by the people (as in Salamonio) or from a further contract – a contract of government (as in the theories, to be discussed below, of Althusius and Pufendorf). Thus the 'contract of society' determines political obligation only if it is treated as a preliminary to the institution of government.

Gierke's distinction is misleading for another reason also: the conceptions of the most important contract theorists do not fall clearly into either of his categories. The contract of Hobbes, for example, is at one and the same time the formation of the state *de novo* by pre-political individuals, *and* (or rather, by means of) the establishment of a government. Because of the latter feature Gierke found himself forced (somewhat uneasily) to place Hobbes among the theorists of the contract of rulership. Locke, on the other hand, he locates (principally) in the other camp, despite the fact that the Lockean contract, like that of Hobbes, establishes civil society by providing for centralised government. As for Rousseau, Gierke viewed him as *entirely* a theorist of the social contract proper, whose most striking innovation, indeed, was the deliberate and explicit suppression of the contract of rulership (GPT, 93,97–8,103–5,109). Yet Rousseau was far from abandoning the contractual vindication of centralised political authority:

just like Hobbes and Locke, he sought to legitimise it as the
outcome of a contract between pre-political individuals. This
essential similarity between the three greatest contract theorists is
obscured by Gierke's schema.

The Reformation

The relation of the Protestant Reformation to political authority
is complex and shifting, and Protestant political theory owed less
to dogma or logic than to the exigencies of varying political
circumstances. There is one obvious exception to this – the role
of the Pope. Clearly for Protestants he could have no role at all,
political or otherwise. Nor did Protestantism replace the Papacy
by any comparable religious authority. Among Protestant writers,
therefore, theories of secular political authority are also theories
of political authority *tout court*. Compared with the Middle Ages,
this was a momentous change in itself. Yet one feature of the
situation inevitably remained constant – the shaping of political
theory by the struggle for power. Often, and understandably,
Protestantism allied itself with secular rulers, who for centuries
had disputed with the Pope the division of European power. But
this was not always the case. In France, in the Netherlands, in
England and in Scotland, Protestantism of the Calvinist variety
found itself engaged in a life-or-death struggle against the ruling
secular authority. All these struggles produced more or less notable
contract theories.

   What appears to be the first of them emerged from the
vicissitudes of the Reformation in England, but its author was not
an Englishman. The Florentine Calvinist Pier Martire Vermigli
(Peter Martyr) came to England in 1547, soon after the inception
of the Protestant regime of Edward VI; in 1553 he fled from that
of Edward's successor, the Catholic Mary Tudor (D'Addio, 1954,
pp.403f.). The experience changed him from an upholder of
monarchical authority, to an advocate of a right of resistance to
monarchs who violate God's law. Vermigli made use of a familiar
kind of contractarian argument – one, indeed, that would scarcely
have surprised Manegold of Lautenbach in the eleventh century.
The authority of kings derives ultimately from God, but the terms

of any ruler's authority are set by contracts between the ruler and the representatives of the people, who elect him to his office on condition that he obeys 'certain laws of the State' (ibid., p.407). If he does not, these electors may compel him to do so by force, or even depose him. In characteristic Calvinist fashion, this corrective function is allotted, not to private individuals or the people as a whole, but to their representatives, the electors, or 'lesser magistrates' – lineal descendants of those German princes whose rights Manegold had championed, on the Pope's behalf, against the Emperor.

Contractarian arguments were congenial to embattled Calvinism. In 1560 the Scottish Reformers succeeded in overthrowing the established Catholic church against the opposition of the secular power, and in 1567 the Protestant nobility forced the abdication of the Catholic Queen Mary. Such an act called for theoretical justification; and this was soon supplied, in the *De Jure Regni apud Scotos*, by the celebrated Scottish scholar and man of letters, George Buchanan. Like Peter Martyr, Buchanan used, among other arguments, the well-worn contractarian one, in much the same old form as Manegold. There is, says Buchanan, a mutual contract between king and people, for on the one hand the people have taken an oath of loyalty to their king, while on the other 'our kings likewise have taken an oath in the presence of our leading men that they will administer the law with fairness and with justice'. Whoever violates his contract, frees the other party from his obligation. A king who upsets the social order is a tyrant and the enemy of his people, against whom they may justly make war (MacNeill, 1964, pp.95–6).

These are familiar arguments. Nevertheless, despite their lack of originality they are of some interest as a harbinger of what was to come. In the conflict-ridden politics of sixteenth century Europe, contract theory was to be found serviceable to more than one cause. Indeed, it was about to enter its classic phase, and in the following two centuries would enjoy a rich conceptual development. It became, perhaps, the central concept of political theory. After Buchanan the torch was next taken up by the French Huguenots in their struggle with the Catholic monarchy of France. It is significant, in this connection, that Salamonio's *De Principatu* was re-published in Paris in 1578;[1] for it was in the following year that there appeared in print the most celebrated of the Huguenot anti-Royalist tracts, and one of the most celebrated of contractarian documents – the *Vindiciae Contra Tyrannos*.

The *Vindiciae* appeared under the pseudonymous authorship of 'Junius Brutus', and its author's real name is not certainly known; however, it is usually attributed to Philippe Duplessis-Mornay, a counsellor close to the Huguenot leader Henry of Navarre (later Henry IV), and that attribution will be followed here. At all events it was written during a bitter religious war, in the aftermath of the massacre of Protestants on St Bartholomew's Eve, 1572.

According to a recent study, the *Vindiciae Contra Tyrannos* is the earliest work of political argument to make 'more than merely casual references' to contracts or covenants (Höpfl and Thompson, 1979, p.929). It should by now be clear that this is scarcely true; nevertheless, it is the case that the use of contractual arguments is probably more insistent in the *Vindiciae* than ever before. What the reason for this might be will emerge shortly. But first we must note that a large part of Duplessis-Mornay's contractarianism is highly traditional, and indeed medieval. 'There is', he wrote, 'a contract mutually obligatory between the king and [his] subjects, which requires the people to obey faithfully, and the king to govern lawfully'. The people are obliged to obey their prince only on this condition: 'if the prince fails in his promise, the people are exempt from obedience, the contract is made void, the right of obligation of no force'. According to Duplessis-Mornay, this is a universal relation, holding 'ever, and in all places'. (LDL, 179,199). Nevertheless, it is clear that his conception of it is the familiar quasi-feudal one. A tyrant, he says, is like a feudal lord who 'transgresses the conditions of his investiture, and is liable to the same punishment'; and he devotes much historical and juridical erudition to showing that in all 'empires, kingdoms and states . . . worthy of the name', rulers on taking office are invested with an authority explicitly conditional on their faithfulness to their investiture oaths – or if not explicitly conditional, tacitly so (LDL, 197,177,181). This quasi-feudal contractarianism of Duplessis-Mornay is not surprising, in view of the fact that the leading Huguenot enemies of the French monarchy were also great feudal magnates.

Yet in spite of all this, the contractarianism of the *Vindiciae* is profoundly original, for the traditional elements are subsumed in a quite new conception, the paradigmatically Calvinist contract

theory. In this respect Duplessis-Mornay contrasts with his predecessors Peter Martyr and Buchanan, whose Calvinism and contractarianism remained essentially separate. In the *Vindiciae*, however,
a characteristically Calvinist note enters when the obligations of
the ruler are described as belonging to his vocation, or divine
calling (LDL, 140). Correspondingly, the contract or covenant
between ruler and people is not simply between ruler and people,
nor is it the only covenant relevant to their relationship. According
to Duplessis-Mornay, the contract between ruler and people
expresses the will of God; God 'has permitted kings to employ
the bodies and the goods of their subjects [both of which are God's
creatures] . . . with this proviso and charge, that they preserve
and defend their subjects' (LDL, 77). Not only this, God is himself
a contractor. Besides the covenant between ruler and people, and
prior to it, is a further covenant, or possibly two covenants,
between God and the ruler, and between God and the people.
The terms of these contracts are pure Calvinist covenant theology;
the king and people undertake 'to honour and serve God according
to His will revealed in His word', and on this condition God
will assist and preserve them, otherwise he will abandon and
exterminate them.[2] It follows that a ruler who destroys true religion
not only may, but must be resisted, and for two reasons: first, that
he is in breach of his covenant with God, on which his rightful
authority depends; second, that the people (or, as we shall see,
their representatives) are obliged by *their* covenant with God to
such resistance (LDL, 71–2,104,109).

Because this theory is built on Calvinist foundations, it is less
than completely universal. Duplessis-Mornay's authority for his
contentions is the Old Testament, and specifically the covenants
it describes as accompanying the inauguration of Hebrew kings
(LDL, 87–9). The covenants with God, therefore, apply only to
rulers and peoples who acknowledge God, that is, to Hebrew and
Christian rulers and peoples. Heathen kings cannot stand in such
a relation to God, though they too are under an obligation to obey
Him, just as if they had covenanted with Him. At this point
Duplessis-Mornay uses an analogy that demonstrates again the
thorough-going interpenetration in his theory of Calvinist and
feudal conceptions; kings – all kings, whether Christian or
heathen – are the vassals of God, and obliged to discharge their
office on the terms laid down by their Lord (LDL, 75–6).

The blending of feudal and Calvinist concepts is manifest again when Duplessis-Mornay discusses what should be done when a ruler flouts this obligation, or otherwise put, transgresses his covenants with God and with the people. Not everyone may or should resist. Private persons should not, for they have no public calling, and everyone must serve God in his own proper calling. The right and responsibility of resistance to princely idolatry and injustice thus falls on those who do have a public calling – the 'lesser magistrates', that is, provincial and municipal governors, and the estates and officers of the kingdom. 'The officers of the kingdom are the guardians and protectors of these covenants and contracts' (LDL, 109–11,199,212). These guardians and protectors are, or include, precisely those great feudatories who were the leaders of the Huguenot party against the French crown. The argument of the *Vindiciae* is at once a defence of true religion, and of the rights of the feudal and provincial nobility.

As one considers the *Vindiciae* and its role in the history of European thought, a paradox appears. All the originality of the *Vindiciae* considered as a contractarian argument is due to Calvinism and the propensity of Calvinism to think of obligations in terms of covenants. Almost certainly it is this propensity, together with the importance of Calvinism in European political conflicts in the sixteenth and seventeenth centuries, that first raised contract theory to the central position it occupied in these and later centuries. Yet the specifically Calvinist elements incorporated in the contract theory of the *Vindiciae* are, one might say, more political theology than political philosophy. Obligations stemming from covenants with God are a matter of faith, not reason. For contract theory to achieve its centrality within secular political thought, this supernatural element had to be, if not eliminated, at least pushed to the sidelines. And, perhaps surprisingly, it was within the ambit of Calvinism itself that this development began.

A case in point is the theory of a later Huguenot, Lambert Daneau (Danaeus). Daneau rested his argument, not on Calvinist theology, but on more or less Aristotelian premises, on to which he grafted a non-Aristotelian, contractarian element (D'Addio, 1954, pp.437–45). Like Aristotle, he saw political communities (states) as the culmination of a series of human associations, starting with the family, and developing through hamlets, villages and towns. But he drew a sharper contrast between paternal power in the family (which in agreement with Aristotle he held to be natural) and political power, which arose from the need to regulate social relations and is constituted by a contract between peoples and their rulers. Thus Daneau may be said to have revived the concept of the original contract (*pactum subiectionis*) in a form not too different from that of Engelbert of Volkersdorf in the fourteenth century, although unlike Engelbert his aim was not to support secular authority but to justify resistance. At the same time he may be seen as a precursor of the greatest of the Calvinist contract theorists, Johannes Althusius.

Gierke claimed that it was Althusius who 'raised the idea of contract to the level of theory' (GPT, 91), and more recent commentators have written similarly that he was the first to use contract as the basis of a 'self-consciously scholarly political theory' (Höpfl and Thompson, 1979, p.935). When we remember the contributions of Manegold and Salamonio, these judgments may seem to rest on a rather narrow conception of theory and scholarliness. None the less, there is no doubting the importance of Althusius for contractarian thought, and it is also true that, unlike his main Calvinist predecessor Duplessis-Mornay (if the latter did indeed write the *Vindiciae*), he was a scholar and a theorist first and foremost. But he was no cloistered and remote academic. After a distinguished career at the Reformed Academy in Herborn, he became in 1604 Syndic of the strongly Calvinist city of Emden in East Friesia, on the border between Germany and the Netherlands. Emden was then deeply involved in struggles with the Lutheran count of East Friesia and the Catholic Emperor; it was also closely allied with the neighbouring Dutch United Provinces, which throughout the closing decades of the sixteenth century were engaged in their own struggle for independence from Catholic Spain, and, after attaining it, still warred with the Spanish Netherlands to the South. As Syndic, Althusius strove, 'with the utmost zeal and enthusiasm, to put his theories into practice' (Gierke). He was, that is, a leading spirit in the struggle for the rights of the burghers against the prince and nobility, and for the Calvinist creed. Although Althusius was a German, his connections with the Netherlands were so close that he may be described as the foremost political theorist of Dutch Calvinism.[3]

Althusius's *magnum opus*, the *Politica Methodice Digesta*, was first published in 1603, but reached its definitive form only in the greatly extended second edition of 1610, which was published at Groningen in the United Provinces. Although original in important ways, it still shows much continuity with earlier arguments, and indeed incorporates wholesale a great deal of the thesis of the *Vindiciae* and, with it, the medieval elements preserved or revived in the latter. For Althusius, as for so many of his predecessors, the authority of the prince or ruler (always referred to by Althusius, in true republican fashion, as the 'supreme magistrate') is constituted and limited by a covenant or contract made between him and the people at the time of his election, which sets the terms of the people's subjection and the prince's rule. Such a contract is a reaffirmation of the *original* contract by which all princely authority was first constituted; 'no realm or commonwealth has ever been founded or instituted except . . . by covenants agreed between subjects and their future prince, and by an established mutual obligation which both should observe. When this obligation is dishonoured, the power of the prince . . . is ended . . .' (PJA, 115,117). According to Althusius, the conditions contained in these covenants, and which are binding on the supreme magistrate, include not only the fundamental laws of the commonwealth, but also, even if not explicitly, the Decalogue. This latter element is a reflection of a higher covenant, that between magistrate and people on the one side and God on the other, in which the human parties have promised to serve, obey, and worship the latter. It is thus a duty of the prince to establish true religion, and of the people's representatives to resist him if he does not; otherwise, they will be 'deservedly punished by God for this fault and surrender, as many examples indicate' (PJA, 157–8,165).

These are all familiar ideas. Althusius's originality lies elsewhere. According to Gierke, Althusius was the first theorist of the contract between rulers and peoples clearly to address himself to the question of what a people is and how it is constituted into a unity capable of being party to a contract (GPT, 91f.). Althusius's account of this owes much to Aristotle; like his predecessor Danaeus he blends Aristotelianism with contractarianism. But his contractarianism is much more thorough-going. He offers a general theory of human association in which contract is a fundamental category.

'The subject-matter of politics', Althusius tells us, 'is association'. Hence it may be called the science of 'symbiotics' (shared life). In such associations, the associates (symbiotes) 'pledge themselves, each to the other, by explicit or tacit agreement'. There are two kinds of such associations, private (for the promotion of private interests) and public. Private associations are brought into existence 'by individual men covenanting among themselves'. They include families, and what Althusius calls the collegium or civil association, which unites 'men of the same trade, training or profession (PJA, 12,22–3,28). Significantly he insists that the private associations are primary, that all others are derived from them, and that they are 'the seedbeds of public association. Human society develops from private to public association'. Public association results from the linking together of many private associations to form 'an inclusive political order' (PJA, 24,34).

Among public associations Althusius distinguishes the particular and the universal. Families and collegia (professional associations) unite to form what Althusius calls a community, a category which embraces hamlets, villages, towns and cities. These are all particular public associations, constituted by 'fixed laws', and their members, Althusius stresses, are not individuals but private associations (PJA, 34–5,37). The same is true of another particular private association, the province, whose members are the 'orders or estates' which in turn are groupings of collegia (or, as Althusius calls them 'greater collegia' – clergy, nobility, burghers, peasants etc.) (PJA, 47,31). Finally, the universal public authority – the realm, commonwealth or people – consists of a number of provinces and cities, united by 'a tacit or express promise' in which they bind themselves 'to hold, organise, use and defend . . . the law of the realm'. Thus a people is constituted, with its own law, and capable of contracting with a future ruler. But the terms of that further contract are already determined by the prior contract by which the realm, and its law, were instituted. It is the people that are sovereign, and the ruler is only their supreme magistrate, charged with administering the laws of the association. In this respect, he is like office-holders in associations in general (PJA, 61–2,115,117, 123,61,66–8,14–15).

We can now see that Althusius's careful blend of individualism and collectivism (or federalism, as it has often been called) provides a rational foundation for the characteristic Calvinist theory of resistance. His theory is individualistic in that its starting-point is the free contracting individual. Nevertheless, it is not individuals that make up the commonwealth or people, but provinces and cities. Provinces and cities retain their rights and laws within the larger political association, and in this sense all states are federal; private associations, too, retain their autonomy within the public associations, which are thus pluralist in their very nature (PJA, 61–2 and *passim*). But the law which binds the prince is the creation, not of individuals, but of the smaller political units that formed the commonwealth. Necessarily, these units must act through representatives or, as Althusius calls them, ephors. Ephors are 'patricians, elders, princes, estates'. They include men who in particular provinces are dukes, princes and counts. Some are 'special ephors', charged with the guardianship of a province or city. It is these ephors who have the function of electing the supreme magistrate, and of enforcing, on behalf of the people, the contract by which his authority was constituted. In the event of his turning tyrant – by violating the fundamental law of the realm, or by administration contrary to justice and piety – the duty of resisting, and if necessary deposing the tyrant, falls to the ephors, or in other words the lesser magistrates (PJA, 94f.,103,110f.,187–90). Althusius does not fail to designate King Philip of Spain as such a tyrant, and the Dutch Wars of Independence levied against him as an example of a proper discharge by ephors of their duties. But, Althusius adds, such a right and duty of resistance 'plainly does not apply to private persons . . . because they do not have the right and use of the sword' (PJA, 186,101,190).

Althusius's theory of associations is in many ways an impressive structure, but it is not free of problems. Compared to the *Vindiciae*, it provides a rationale for resistance which is much less dependent on Calvinist theology. This it achieves by virtue of what may be called a 'contractualised' version of Aristotle, in which the Aristotelian series of human groups is made to depend on successive contracts. This, however, creates some theoretical strains. For Althusius adopts Aristotle's view that man is political *by nature*, a naturally gregarious animal who cannot live alone, so that the commonwealth 'exists by nature', yet at the same time holds that 'in the beginning of the human race there were neither imperia nor realms' – 'families, cities and provinces existed by nature prior to realms' (PJA, 13,19,90,61). Perhaps there is no contradiction here – rather, what is natural is realised in the course of a historical process. But Althusius's Aristotelian federalism encounters serious difficulties when he tries to combine it with a concept of sovereignty taken over from the French theorist Jean Bodin. Bodin is celebrated in the history of political thought as the founder of the concept of the absolute sovereignty of rulers. As such, he is explicitly recognised as an enemy by Althusius, who maintains, to the contrary, that sovereignty inheres in the commonwealth, that is, the people (PJA, 66–7). But if cities and provinces precede commonwealths in time, it is hard to see why they, in their time, would not also have been sovereign – in effect, independent commonwealths. Althusius did not manage to achieve a consistent position on provinces – on whether they are by definition parts of a larger whole, or have had a previous history of independence. Indeed, not until the second edition of the *Politica* did he maintain the latter (PJA, 46). Rather uneasily, he remarks that provincial governors receive their trust 'from the realm under which the province exists', yet 'have rights of sovereignty in their territory' (PJA, 56–7). This surely is incoherent, and it is an incoherence at a crucial point of the theory, on which Althusius's specification of the right of resistance depends.

Social contract theory and the Counter-Reformation

It was suggested above that the rise of social contract theory in early modern Europe was largely due to the political importance of Calvinism, plus the affinity between contractualist thinking and aspects of Calvinist theology. That is not to say, however, that contract theory was confined to Calvinist thinkers – on the contrary, it is to suggest that through these thinkers it was transmitted to political thought in general, including the thought of Calvinism's enemies.

Their bitterest enemies, naturally, were the extreme Catholics, and it should not be particularly surprising to find the latter, in their turn, resorting to contractarian arguments. There were, after all, plenty of medieval precedents. All that was necessary for these precedents to be revived was an appropriate political situation. In France, the change in political fortunes consequent on the accession of Henri IV (previously the leader of the Huguenots) produced a kind of reversal of intellectual allegiances; Duplessis-Mornay became a leading minister, while the role of champions of the right of resistance passed to the bitterest enemies of the Huguenots, the Catholic League. Several League publicists justified this right in terms of the contract between king and people (Allen, 1960, p.347). But more important for political thought than the propagandists of the League were the theorists of that intellectual spearhead of the Counter-Reformation, the Society of Jesus.

Two of the Jesuits in particular merit attention here. Both are Spaniards. One is Fernando Vasquez, author of two treatises, the *Controversiarum Usu Frequentium* and the *Illustrium Controversiarum Aliarumque Frequentium*. By a very different route, Vasquez arrived at conclusions in some ways similar to those of his great contemporary and enemy, Althusius. Where Althusius drew on Calvinist, Aristotelian and feudal ideas, Vasquez's main sources were St Augustine and Roman law. The latter authority makes his work seem, in part, like a revival of Salamonio. To Vasquez, as to Salamonio, the law of the state is a contract between the citizens, by which the prince is bound. Once again, the basis of princely authority is the *lex regia*, by which the people (if they so choose) delegate authority, on conditions, to their prince. To Vasquez (here going further than Salamonio) this conditional delegation is also a contract, the contract between people and ruler – the same contract, according to Vasquez, as Augustine had referred to: *generale pactum societatis humanae obtemperare Principibus* (the general contract of human society to obey their kings) (D'Addio, 1954, pp.450–57). Thus in Vasquez, as in Althusius, there are two kinds of contracts, the one constituting the state, the other the prince. On the other hand a great difference must be noted between Vasquez on the one hand, and Althusius, the Calvinists and Salamonio on the other: while the latter diminished the authority of kings in order to exalt the rights of subjects, Vasquez did so in order to exalt the authority of the Pope. In this he is of course typical of the Jesuits, and similar to medieval papalists such as Manegold of Lautenbach.

An interesting further feature of Vasquez's argument is his account of the pre-political state of man, which draws on the ideas of the Christian Fathers. Men are by nature free, and at first lived free from legal and political obligation; but they fell into disorder, and so found it necessary to institute political authority for the sake of peace and justice (ibid., p.450–53). It was Vasquez's fellow-Jesuit, Juan de Mariana, who gave the most elaborate account so far of this pre-political condition. At one time, he says, men lived much like animals, in separate families, and in a condition of innocence. Their weaknesses and needs led them to associate in groups, this involved the recognition of property rights and, as a consequence, increasing greed, cheating and lying – a veritable war of all against all.[4] Government was instituted as the remedy. While Mariana is scarcely a contract theorist (apart from a brief reference to men 'binding themselves together with others by a compact of society'), his concern with the condition of pre-political man is a feature in common with the great contract theorists of the next two centuries, and in that sense he is their precursor.

4 Social Contract Theory in Seventeenth-Century Britain

Throughout the seventeenth century the peace of Europe continued to be disturbed by religious quarrels stemming from the Reformation, as well as the habitual struggles for power between kings and their enemies; and in the arguments provoked by these disturbances the theory of social contract provided a widely accepted idiom, perhaps more widely accepted than ever before or since. At any rate this was so in Britain, where the century was not only the 'century of genius', but also the century of Civil War and 'Glorious' Revolution. Not that the social contract theory was universally accepted – by and large, it was found much more congenial by the enemies of established authority than by its friends. But to that generalisation there stands a towering exception – Thomas Hobbes.

In accounting for the popularity of the contractualist idiom in seventeenth century Britain, many commentators have pointed, rightly, to the influence of that peculiarly English brand of Calvinist or quasi-Calvinist Protestantism, Puritanism, and especially those Puritan groups that found it necessary to separate from the established church. In addition to the usual Calvinist covenant theology, these groups were disposed to think in contractarian terms by the very process of establishing their voluntary churches; and this disposition was able, in some circumstances, to find political application, as in the famous case of the Pilgrim Fathers.[1] But the Fathers' declared intent to 'solemnly and mutually, in the presence of God and of one another, covenant and combine ourselves together into a civil body politic', while certainly a social contract, is not a statement of social contract *theory*. Nor is that other famous document of Puritan contractualism, the Agreement of the People,[2] drawn up in 1648 and 1649 by the Levellers, the radical democratic party in the English Civil War, which was a *proposed* contract, designed to establish a national constitution, and to be signed, not by all subjects, but only by the 'well-affected people' and their representatives, though it would be binding on all. Interesting though these phenomena are, they are peripheral to our subject.

Let us, therefore, turn our attention to the use made of social contract *theory* in political argument in seventeenth-century Britain. Broadly speaking, we may distinguish three types of users: men of affairs, political propagandists, and philosophers (Hobbes and Locke). These distinctions are not intended to suggest that the philosophers were politically neutral or 'objective' or even uninvolved in practical politics; rather, they point to differences in the quality and style of argument, which quite clearly distinguish the philosophers from the others, from the propagandists or pamphleteers as much as from the men of affairs. Indeed, the ideas deployed by the politicians and the pamphleteers are so similar that they can be treated together, and it is remarkable how little the philosophical arguments affected them.

The resort by politicians and propagandists to contractarian argument was a consequence, in the first instance, of the Civil War, or Great Rebellion, which tore Britain apart in mid-century. Thanks to the Union of the Crowns in 1603, Charles I inherited the thrones of both Scotland and England; by 1642, his policies, and notably his religious policies, had provoked rebellion in both kingdoms, with the Scottish Presbyterians and English Puritans equally prominent among the king's enemies. Justifications by the rebels of their action began to appear in print almost immediately, and once again contractarian arguments were to the fore. That history should thus repeat itself has its own considerable significance; none the less, the theoretical interest of most of these polemics is slight, and they can be dealt with rather briefly, for they have little claim to originality. Thus, for example, the English anti-royalist pamphleteer Charles Herle was content to invoke yet again the venerable doctrine of a 'paction' between king and people (Herle, 1642, p.6). A more developed contract argument is provided by the Scottish Presbyterian divine Samuel Rutherford in his *Lex Rex*, but he does little more than repeat the argument

of the *Vindiciae contra Tyrannos* (Rutherford, 1644, esp. p.96f).
His reliance on 'Junius Brutus' is explicit). A rather more original
argument is that of John Milton, poet, Puritan, and republican, in
his *Tenure of Kings and Magistrates*. Somewhat in the manner of
Jesuits such as Vasquez and Mariana, Milton added to an orthodox
Christian account of the condition of pre-political, post-lapsarian
man, a more or less contractual account of the origin of commonwealths:

> 'From the root of Adam's transgression, falling among themselves
> to do wrong and violence, and foreseeing that such courses must
> needs tend to the destruction of them all, they agreed by
> common league to bind each other from mutual injury, and
> jointly to defend themselves against any that gave disturbance
> or opposition to such agreement.'

Later they found it necessary to enforce the agreement by
delegating or entrusting authority to do so to kings and magistrates;
later still, the latter having been corrupted by power, to recall
them to their trust by establishing definite laws; and finally to
make their allegiance to their rulers explicitly conditional, by
means of a 'bond or covenant', on the rulers' enforcing and
respecting the laws. Thus Milton invokes once again the contract
between ruler and people, but this time it is depicted as a remedy
for previous breaches of trust on the ruler's part. However, Milton
later goes on to assert that the people is entitled to depose a ruler
at will, even though he be 'no tyrant', so it does not look as if he
took this contract very seriously (Milton, 1974, pp.255–6,259).

As the examples of Herle, Rutherford and Milton indicate, the
ancient doctrine of the contract between king and people continued
to be attractive to the British opponents of royal power during the
Civil War, just as it had been to their equivalents in previous
centuries. This was even more the case during the later crisis which
culminated in the second expulsion of the Stuarts in 1688, and in
which Puritanism was far less salient. It is thus not surprising that
the doctrine was condemned in 1683 by the staunchly royalist
University of Oxford (Ritchie, 1893, p.209 fn 1). The condemnation
had little efficacy, however. In the Parliamentary debates preceding
the fall of King James, the king's Whig enemies made continual
reference to the 'pact' or 'covenant' with the people on which

government is based. 'Government' said Sir Henry Capel 'is a mutual compact between the intended governor and those that are to be governed'. The House of Lords itself was moved to ask some distinguished lawyers to explain the meaning of 'the original contract', and received the answer that it must refer to 'the first original of government'. And on 29 January 1689 the House of Commons resolved that, King James 'having endeavoured to subvert the Constitution of the Kingdom by breaking the Original Contract between king and people', the throne had therefore become vacant.[3] With the Whig victory of 1689, the doctrine of the original contract became part of official ideology. It was neatly summarised in an anonymous pamphlet, 'The Revolution Vindicated':

'By the Original Contract [is] meant the agreement that had always been between the kings and people of England, that the government should be a legal government ... The coronation oath, and the oath of allegiance, are the seals of this contract ... The constitution comprehends the particular form and nature of the legal government in which the king and people are at any time agreed; which was the same with the Original Contract at first, and was expressed in the ancient fundamental laws.' (Kenyon, 1977, p.43)

The only slight originality of these ideas lies in their parochialism; they express, not a theory of government as such, but a theory of the English government, whose authority is derived from a contract identified with the ancient constitution of the realm.

Hobbes

While English politicians of the seventeenth century and their propagandists were content to rehearse yet again the time-honoured contractarian ideas, English philosophers were spurred by the political crises of the age to give contract theory its classic expression. Already political philosophy, in the person of Althusius, had moved well beyond the version of contract theory that appealed to practical men. Our task now is to delineate briefly the development of ideas between Althusius and Thomas Hobbes.

Hobbes's version of the social contract theory is philosophically the most impressive of all. It is also the most innovative, both philosophically and politically. Politically, it is highly unusual in that it used contract theory to defend and uphold the authority of rulers, indeed a (nearly) absolute authority. Of all the many previous contract theorists we have surveyed, only one – Engelbert of Volkersdorf – was also a supporter of secular authority (that of the Emperor), and even he can hardly be said to have *used* contract theory much or very convincingly to that end. Philosophically, Hobbes was just as original, and in too many ways to yield to easy summary. But even the most original ideas have antecedents, and some of these must now be considered.

In some ways Hobbes is philosophically closer to Salamonio than to his more recent predecessor, Althusius. To the more or less Aristotelian Althusius, there was no such thing as a pre-political state of man; man is by nature a political animal, and his state was always political, even if it took some time before his political nature achieved *full* realisation in the commonwealth. To Salamonio, drawing more on ideas inherited from Roman law and pre-Reformation Christian thought, individuals are by nature not only equal (as Althusius also held) but also free, and once exercised their natural liberty in a pre-political state. The same view was held by the Jesuit writer Vasquez (discussed above), and was indeed typical of the Jesuit theorists in general, including the most notable of them, Francisco Suarez.[4] But Suarez not only held that men, in a pre-political state, were naturally free; he also held that this freedom was a *natural right*, and that it was by virtue of their right over their natural liberty that men were able to establish government, through a contract of the familiar kind between a people and their ruler. In other words, just because man's natural freedom is a natural right, it can be alienated. Suarez is not specific as to the terms and conditions of this alienation, that is, of the contract of government, but he is clear that whatever these may have been, men are obliged to keep their contracts. Whereas to an earlier writer such as Salamonio this obligation stemmed from the *ius gentium* (human law), to Suarez it was a principle of natural law (*ius naturale*) – indeed, the earlier distinction between these two types of law had by Suarez's time begun to drop out of sight GNL, 38,233–4). A generation after Suarez wrote, a view very similar to his on the natural right of liberty and its contractual alienation to a ruler or government was expressed by the celebrated Dutch theorist Hugo Grotius in his *De Jure Belli et Pacis*. Grotius, like Suarez, declined to specify any necessary terms of this alienation, but was explicit that it *might* be total:

> 'From the Jewish as well as the Roman Law, it appears that any one might engage himself in private servitude to whom he pleased. Now if an individual may do so, why may not a whole people, for the benefit of better government and more certain protection, completely transfer their sovereign rights to one or more persons, without reserving any portion to themselves?'[5]

Again, similar views on the original contract of government as a (possibly total) alienation of natural rights were held by the English humanist scholar and legal theorist John Selden, who was Grotius's contemporary (and, in other respects, his opponent) (Tuck, 1979, pp.86,90–100). Selden is also of interest in holding that, at a period *before* the promulgation of natural law (by God), man's natural right of liberty was itself total, that is, unfettered by any obligation whatever – and that in this period men lived 'like animals, sustaining a bestial existence and managing their lives by brute force rather than reason'. He thus united the old humanistic picture of man's primitive condition (see pp.25,27 above) with a (non-humanist) conception of natural rights. Equally significant is the relation postulated by Selden between natural rights and natural law; whereas for Suarez the (limited) natural right of liberty was a concomitant of the law of nature, Selden's (unlimited) natural right is in opposition to natural law, for the primeval, unlimited natural right is anarchic and anti-social.

When Selden applied his conception of the original contract to the English case, it made him, in the context of the political struggles that culminated in the Civil War, a defender of the concept of the 'balanced' constitution and of the liberties of subjects, and in general of Parliament against the king. Nevertheless, it is not hard to see how his ideas might be found serviceable by upholders of royal power. A case in point is his contemporary Sir Dudley Digges (d.1643), a leading member of the celebrated Tew Circle. The right of nature, wrote Digges in *The Unlawfulness of Subjects taking up Arms*, was an unlimited freedom, common to all mankind, 'to use our abilities, according as will did prompt', which led inevitably to 'fears and jealousies, wherein every single person looked upon the world as his enemy'. To escape this situation, and for the sake of self-preservation, 'we voluntarily and upon agreement restrained our selves from making use of this native right . . . Reason induced men to enter into such a Covenant, and to lay mutual obligation one upon another, not to resent authority upon whatever grounds', even including 'real injustice' (ibid., pp.102–4). Thus, Digges used a contractual argument in support of absolute non-resistance to authority; he did not, however, go so far as to ground that authority itself on contract, a stance presumably uncongenial to royalist thoughtways, but relied on Divine right. The fashioning of a fully contractual theory of absolute or near-absolute authority was thus left to Thomas Hobbes.

Hobbes was born in 1588 and was thus over 50 when the Civil War broke out in England. But for this cataclysm he might well never have turned his attention to political theory. His earlier intellectual interests lay elsewhere – in the study of the classics (he published a notable translation of Thucydides), and later in the new philosophy and science of the seventeenth century. Many years were spent in the service of aristocratic families, as tutor. The threatened outbreak of hostilities between the king and his enemies induced in him two responses. One was to work out his political philosophy – a philosophy of peace. The other was to flee from the war, first to Paris, where for a while he served as tutor to the future Charles II. But in 1651, after the defeat of the Royalists, he returned to England and submitted to the regime of Oliver Cromwell. After the Restoration of Charles II in 1660, Hobbes too was restored to the favour of his former tutee. But many of the king's supporters did not share his benevolent view of Hobbes – to them he was a turn-coat, and his philosophy was a turn-coat philosophy, dishonourable and even dangerous. In a sense they were right. Hobbes would – and did – come to terms with whoever was in power. But this was a matter, not of opportunism, but of principle. His commitment was not to any party, but to peace. The rebellious Cromwell of 1642 was a disturber of the peace, the victorious Cromwell of 1651 its only possible preserver. Hobbes's behaviour was utterly consistent with his philosophy, the essentials of which never changed.

Hobbes's greatest work, the *Leviathan*, also dates from 1651, though earlier formulations of his political philosophy go back to 1640.[6] As a theory of social contract, it out-classes all its predecessors as a structure of systematic and rigorous argument. (Only Althusius's *Politica* approaches it on this plane, but Althusius is far inferior to Hobbes in style and wit.) Perhaps the most immediately striking and innovative feature of Hobbes's argument is that he dispenses completely, and designedly, with the familiar idea of a contract between ruler and people. Salamonio, alone among earlier contract theorists, spoke only of a pact among individual citizens, and in this respect is somewhat like Hobbes. But Salamonio's pact established the laws of the state, by which political authority is bound, whereas the Hobbesian contract, also among individuals, establishes political authority directly, prior to civil law, and indeed as the source of that law.

Despite its originality, Hobbes's theory naturally makes use of many familiar elements. Like many of his predecessors, he develops his argument on political obligation through a contrast between the political and the pre-political condition of man. He is thus concerned with the origin of government, and so his theory is a theory of the 'original contract'. The pre-political state of man is unequivocally designated by Hobbes as 'the *natural* condition of mankind' and the 'state of *nature*' (emphases added) – political society, in other words, is not natural to men (contrary to Aristotle), but the result of 'art'.[7] To the depiction of men's natural, pre-political condition, Hobbes devotes unprecedented care and rigour. We have seen that for many writers, stretching back through the Jesuits and Salamonio to the Christian Fathers, men are by nature equal and free. With this Hobbes agrees. In his eyes, however, this fact is by no means advantageous; nor does it entail limits on political authority (as for Salamonio and so many others) but rather the reverse.

In a sense, the freedom and equality of men in a state of nature is a tautology. If there is no political authority, each individual is *de facto* and *de jure* free from such authority and each has the same political (or rather, non-political) status. The political institutions that create restrictions and discriminations are by definition lacking. But natural freedom and equality mean more than this to Hobbes (as to his predecessors, though differently). Let us first consider man's natural equality. To Hobbes, this is in the first place a fact of human nature, in an empirical, descriptive sense. All human beings are essentially alike, and their likeness determines their political predicament. They are creatures of action and of passion, and their actions depend on their passions – on two kinds of passion, called by Hobbes desires and aversions. The objects of a man's desire cause him pleasure, the objects of his aversion, displeasure. Thus our actions are the seeking, not exactly of pleasure, but of objects that give us pleasure, and the shunning of whatever gives us displeasure or pain (HL, 118–19, 122). Human life, then, is a continual seeking to satisfy desires: 'Life itself ... can never be without desire'. And 'the felicity of this life' is nothing but 'continual success in obtaining those things which a man from time to time desireth'. There is, says Hobbes, 'no such thing as perpetual tranquility of mind, while we live here' (HL, 129–30). Man, as a desiring but also a reasoning creature, must be of necessity preoccupied with the means of achieving his desires; that is, says Hobbes, with his *power*. 'The power of a man (to take it universally), is his present means, to obtain some future apparent good'. Hence man is by nature a maximiser of his power. 'I put for a general inclination of all mankind, a perpetual and restless desire of power after power, that ceaseth only in death' (HL, 150,161).

That men are intrinsically power-seekers hints at their political predicament, for one form of power is power over other men. Human life is thus apt to be a struggle for power. But the predicament is enormously intensified by another aspect of human equality, that of body and mind.

> 'Nature hath made men so equal, in the faculties of body, and mind, [that] the weakest has strength enough to kill the strongest, either by secret machination, or by confederacy with others ... From this equality of ability, ariseth equality of hope in the attaining of our ends. And therefore if any two men desire the same thing, which nevertheless they cannot both enjoy, they become enemies; and in the way to their end ... endeavour to destroy or subdue one another.' (HL, 183–4)

The natural relation of men, therefore, is competitive, and their competition has no natural limit as to the means employed. Hence their relation is also one of mutual fear (diffidence, in Hobbes's term) – fear of destruction by rivals and enemies, leading to what

Hobbes calls 'anticipation' – that is, attack as the best form of self-defence. Competition and diffidence, says Hobbes, are two 'principal causes of quarrel,' which makes the natural condition of mankind a war 'of every man, against every man' (HL, 184–5).

The war is further intensified by one particular, in Hobbes's view, pre-eminent human desire – the desire for glory. Glorying is 'joy, arising from imagination of a man's own power and ability', and this passion too is antisocial. For its gratification demands recognition by others of one's eminence:

> 'Every man looketh that his companion should value him, at the same rate he sets upon himself: And upon all signs of contempt, or undervaluing, naturally endeavours, as far as he dares (which amongst them that have no common power, to keep them in quiet, is far enough to make them destroy each other,) to extort a greater value from his contemners.' (HL, 124–5,185)

Hobbes even went so far as to claim on one occasion, that 'all the mind's pleasure is either glory, ... or refers to glory in the end' (HC, 24). There can be little doubt that Hobbes attributed the misfortune of the English Civil War, in large measure, to a desire for glory, on the part of the rebels and others.

One other feature of human nature seems equally, indeed more obviously, implicated in this disaster – man's religiosity. Man is by nature religious. This is because he is a reasoning, but a largely ignorant creature. He is able to discover relations of cause and effect, and to think of all phenomena as the effects of causes, yet of the causes of very many phenomena he is ignorant. He therefore attributes them to invisible powers – spirits and gods. Since any power is a potential threat, he also fears these entities, and seeks to placate or even control them by worship etc. – that is, by religion. Hobbes points out the enormous number of forms human religion has taken, and the huge variety of objects of human worship. There is, says Hobbes, a true religion, but the great majority of human religions are false. Among the latter, Hobbes implies, are the Church of Rome and the most advanced Reformed churches – in English terms, the Puritans (HL, chapter XII). Though Hobbes does not actually say so, one may wonder if he did not mean to imply that human religiosity is a further cause of quarrel among men. Not only would Hobbes's experience of the

Civil War have led him to think so, but it is also striking that in the *Leviathan* the chapter 'Of Religion' immediately precedes the chapter 'Of the Natural Condition of Mankind', which describes and explains the war of every man against every man.

Let us turn from religion to morality. There is, in Hobbes's view, a true, universal morality, derivable from the nature of man, and expressed in the laws of nature. The status of these laws, about which students of Hobbes have spilt much ink, seems actually clear enough, if not simple. On the one hand, they hold the key to peace and orderly human society; but on the other, in the natural condition of mankind – the war of every man against every man – many though not all of them are inoperative. As laws, they entail obligations, and in a state of war and universal fear, where no one can be trusted, it is neither possible nor rational for a man to accept obligations. Hence Hobbes's conception of the right of nature (that is, the right of men in the state of nature) which, like that of some earlier writers, is a right of total liberty – in Hobbes's famous phrase, 'every man has a right to every thing; even to one another's body' (HL, 189–90).[8] By this, Hobbes means a right to get everything he can get, and do everything he can do – for in the war of every man against every man, 'nothing can be unjust. The notions of right and wrong, justice and injustice, have there no place'. There is, to be sure, a place for the notions of good and evil: men call the objects of their desire 'good' and the objects of their aversion 'evil. But these judgements are purely subjective, and conflicting in so far as man's desires conflict. Indeed they intensify the conflict of the state of nature. Little wonder that the life of man therein is 'solitary, poor, nasty, brutish and short' (HL, 188,120,186).

If such was the natural condition of men, the consequence of their natural liberty and equality, it is not surprising that they chose to leave it. Men are creatures of passion, but also reasoning creatures. Certain passions, says Hobbes, incline men to peace – for example, 'desire of such things as are necessary to commodious living; and a hope by their industry to obtain them'; and also – above all – fear of death. 'And reason suggesteth convenient Articles of Peace, upon which men may be drawn to agreement. These Articles are they which otherwise are called the Laws of Nature'. A law of nature, Hobbes goes on to explain, is 'a precept or general rule, found out by reason, by which a man is forbidden to do that which is destructive of his life, or taketh away the means of preserving the same; and to omit that by which he thinketh it may be best preserved.' The laws of nature, therefore, which are the true universal morality, also correspond to the self-interest and especially the common interest of men (HL, 188,189,215–16). Particularly important are three laws of nature: first, and most fundamentally, 'That every man ought to endeavour peace, as far as he has hope of obtaining it'; secondly (derived from the first), for the sake of peace, that he be 'willing to lay down [the natural] right to all things; and be contented with so much liberty against other men, as he would allow other men against himself'; thirdly, 'that men perform their covenants made' (HL, 190, 201). In sum, men must, for the sake of peace, make a contract or covenant to renounce their natural liberty, and they must abide by this covenant. The notion of an obligation to abide by one's promise or contract is of course a corner-stone of all social contract theory, and there is nothing new in supposing such an obligation to be a law of nature; but that Hobbes should portray the *making* of the contract as also an obligation of natural law is indeed a striking innovation, and a testimony to Hobbes's revolutionary interpretation of that old phrase.

As stated above, most laws of nature are inoperative in the state of nature, but the first two are exceptions. In effect, they impose an obligation to leave the state of nature, if possible. In a sense they are an exception to the unfettered liberty of that state, for if a man is offered the opportunity to leave the state of nature and enter orderly society he is not at liberty to decline the offer. He is not at liberty to decline to be a party to the covenant by which Leviathan, the Commonwealth, can be established. As for the other laws of nature, in the state of nature, as Hobbes puts it, they 'oblige *in foro interno*; that is to say, they bind to a desire they should take place': but not *in foro externo*, that is, as to the actual act (HL, 215).[9] One is thus obliged always to seek a situation – one of peace – where the laws of nature are fully obligatory. The covenant of renunciation by which men may pass from the state of nature to ordered society is thus fully binding because, even although made in a state of nature, it falls to be observed in ordered society – even if, paradoxically, the very existence of ordered society depends on its being observed.

It is now time to take a closer look at this covenant. That the making of it is obligatory under the law of nature does not mean only, for Hobbes, that it is a moral obligation; it means also that it is a necessity of man's nature, an act that men, as passionate and reasoning creatures, must be presumed to have indeed performed. Strictly speaking, this act is, in Hobbes's terminology, a contract – a mutual transferring of right – in the form of multilateral covenants (to covenant is to promise, as party to a contract, some performance in the future). The second law of nature (see above) hints at what its terms must be – a renunciation of natural right. But this in itself is insufficient, for it fails to deal with the fundamental cause of the miseries of the state of nature – the lack of a 'common power' sufficient to keep men 'in awe', and thus to preserve peace. Men must authorise (must have authorised) a *sovereign* to govern them, 'as if every man should say to every man, "I authorise and give up my right of governing myself to this man, or to this assembly of men, on this condition, that thou give up thy right to him, and authorise all his actions in like manner" ' (HL, 192–3,225,227). As is very clear, the sovereign ruler is no party to this contract and has no obligations under it: the contracting parties are the future citizens of the commonwealth, and each one has, by this contract, a dual obligation to obey the sovereign – each one has transferred his right of self-government to the sovereign, who thereby has the right to rule him; and each has made a promise to this effect to his fellow-citizens, and is obliged to them to obey the sovereign, if they do.

Hobbes's startling innovation here is to produce a legitimate political authority directly out of the contract of individuals made in a state of nature. Here is no contract between ruler and people, nor (as in Salamonio) a contract between citizens *prior* to the institution of authority. Hence Hobbes is enabled to give his ruler an extremely wide (if not totally unrestricted) authority. The establishing of a ruler (or ruling assembly, though this to Hobbes is less preferable because a less effective way of maintaining order) is, as Hobbes stresses, an authorisation: that is, every contractor authorises 'all the actions and judgments, of that man, or that assembly of men . . . as if they were his own'. The sovereign is thus the representative of all citizens of the commonwealth, and its only source of unity (HL, 241f.,228–9,220). The consequences of this unification and authorisation are dramatic indeed. Not only has the sovereign acquired full rights of governing, including the right to make the civil law (which is the sovereign's command); he has also acquired other rights that men were at liberty to exercise in the state of nature, such as the right to judge good and evil. There is now an objective standard of value. In the commonwealth, 'the measure of good and evil actions, is the civil law'. Not only is there no right to disobey the sovereign's law, there is no right to criticise it. Similarly, the sovereign has the right to enforce his interpretation of true religion. After all, by the contract, 'every subject is author of the actions of his sovereign', and every 'action and judgement' of the sovereign is to be taken as the action and judgement of every citizen. To be sure, the laws of nature are eternal moral truths, but there is no possibility of appealing to these laws against the civil laws, for it is the first and fundamental law of nature that leads to the authorisation of the sovereign. 'The Law of Nature and the Civil Law contain each other, and are of equal extent'. If this version of social contract theory seems to give excessive power to rulers and to endanger their subjects, Hobbes has a simple answer: 'Sovereign power [is] not so hurtful as the want of it' (HL, 312–13,365,333, 232,314,238).

As a matter of fact, Hobbes's position is not so extreme as it may seem. True, the sovereign has, according to him, absolute authority to rule, and is responsible for his exercise of authority to no one but God. Nevertheless, the obligation of the subject to obey the sovereign is not unlimited. As Hobbes remarks, a covenant is a voluntary act: 'and of the voluntary acts of every man, the object is some *good to himself.* And therefore there be some rights, which no man can . . . have abandoned, or transferred', notably his right to defend his 'own body'. The transfer of natural right to the sovereign, therefore, is subject to this exception, and it follows that no one is obliged, in obedience to the sovereign, 'to kill, wound or maim himself; or not to resist those that assault him; or to abstain from the use of food, air, medicine, or any other thing, without which he cannot live', or even, in certain cases, to fight in the sovereign's wars (HL, 260,376,192,268–9). A man may always defend his life and person, even against the sovereign – a conclusion that seems to follow necessarily from Hobbes's premises. But – consistently with these premises – 'no man hath liberty to resist the sword of the Commonwealth, in defence of another man' (HL, 270), for such a liberty would destroy the sovereign's necessary power, whereas the liberty of self-defence alone does not.

All obligation of obedience, indeed, depends on the sovereign's power, and when he loses it, he loses his authority also. Our obligation is always to the ruler with effective power (on which peace depends). A sovereign who acquires power by force, possibly by overthrowing a previous government, has exactly the same authority, and is owed the same obligation, as a sovereign established by an original or other contract (HL, 272,252). The rationale of his authority is exactly the same, and the fact that he may have acquired his power by illegal and unjust means – means which Hobbes unreservedly condemns – is irrelevant. It was doctrines such as these that permitted Hobbes to rally to Cromwell in 1651, and made him so suspect to royalists and political traditionalists generally.

Though Hobbes's theory pleased no party in the political struggles of seventeenth century England, the magnitude of his theoretical achievement is apparent. Starting from all the usual premises employed by his opponents to restrict the authority of rulers – the primacy of the law of nature, the natural liberty and equality of man, the dependence of political authority on a social contract – he produced, with impressive logic, exactly the contrary conclusion. But this, perhaps, is the least of his originality. Even more striking is the way Hobbes integrated contract theory into the most advanced philosophical developments of his age – the age of Descartes and Galileo (whom Hobbes met in 1636), and of the first stages of the scientific revolution. Hobbes aimed at a *science* of politics, a body of *demonstrated* universal propositions, going beyond wisdom and experience, proved as conclusively as the propositions of Euclid.[10] To establish the premises of his demonstration, Hobbes followed the method of Paduan natural science, the method of 'resolution and composition'. The object of study – the commonwealth – was broken down (resolved) into parts – men – and reconstituted (composed) – by deduction from premises about men, or premises of human nature (cf. Peters, 1956, pp.64–5,158). Furthermore, men were conceived by Hobbes in a thoroughly materialistic and deterministic fashion, as if they consisted purely of material particles governed by scientific laws (this, naturally, was a further scandal to orthodox opinion). In this respect Hobbes seems to have been quite original – even Descartes had postulated materialism only for animals, adding in the human case a second, distinct substance – the soul. But Hobbes explained human passions and actions wholly as the outcome of matter in motion. Actions, to him, are indeed bodily motions – voluntary motions – and desires and aversions are not only their causes but their 'small beginnings'. Desire and aversion, in turn, depend on pleasure and displeasure; and objects which cause pleasure and desire are those that aid what Hobbes calls our 'vital motion', while those that cause displeasure and aversion hinder it (HL, 118–19,121–2). In brief, all our actions are determined by the effects of objects on our physiological well-being.

Hobbes's intellectual audacity is remarkable, but in several respects problematic. He wished to demonstrate that for every human being, obedience to the sovereign is a necessary deduction from his (or her) very nature. For this he relies, crucially, on the postulate that every human being's strongest passion is necessarily aversion to death. But must it be? Was the Civil War due purely to men's failure to appreciate their true interest? What of those who might have claimed that their strongest passion was a desire for eternal bliss in a life after death, or to glorify God? Hobbes's answer is that God commands the laws of nature, and thereby obedience to the sovereign (HL, 217). But this really introduces into the argument an extraneous element out of keeping with its general tenor.

It has also been suggested by some commentators – notably Patrick Riley in a recent book (Riley 1982, pp.9–11,15–16 and chapter 2) that Hobbes's synthesis of contract theory and scientific determinism is an uneasy one. The fundamental premise of tradition-al contract theory is that men are bound by their promise. Hobbes agrees with this premise. But is he really entitled to? The orthodox notion of this moral obligation is that it arises from the fact that a promise is an exercise of a person's free choice. Hobbes speaks often enough of liberty and freedom, but he means thereby only the absence of physical and legal *restriction*, not the absence of physical necessitation (HL, 261–3).[11] It is dubious whether this allows for a sufficient genuineness of choice to found a moral obligation. But be this as it may, Hobbes's method does have one great advantage, from his point of view: it removes all scope for questioning whether men are parties to the contract of sovereignty, for this is not a matter in which they have any option. As noted above, they are obliged *to* the contract, as well as *by* the contract. Thus Hobbes does not have to face the problem, so troublesome to Locke and other theorists of the original contract, as to the obligations of later generations of subjects. Just as no one has any option but to submit to a conqueror, so no one, when he reaches the age of majority, has any option but to accept the authority of any existing commonwealth in which he lives.[12]

But Hobbes's synthesis of contract theory and scientific method raises (or reinforces) another problem. If Hobbes's theory is a deduction from human nature (as he says, an 'inference made from the passions'), can it also be a historical account? Is Hobbes really claiming that the state of nature and the contract are actual historical occurrences, by which men passed from a pre-political to a political condition? Many commentators have urged that, to the contrary, the state of nature is a kind of fiction or hypothetical model, showing what the condition of men *would* be like (or *is* like) in the absence of government, and the contract is a depiction of the terms that *would* (or should) be acceptable to all men in such a condition, and therefore should be acceptable to all men quite generally.[13] There is some warrant for this interpretation in Hobbes's text, but overall it seems to me clear that his argument requires that the state of nature and the contract be (as for his predecessors) genuine historical phenomena. Not only does Hobbes refer to the state of nature, more than once, as being '*before* the erection of a Commonwealth', and by similar phrases, and likewise to 'the pacts and covenants, by which the parts of [the] Body Politic were *first* made', and so on; even more importantly, he continually relies on the actuality of promise as the foundation of men's political obligation. Thus: 'Every subject in a Commonwealth, *hath covenanted* to obey the Civil Law ... And therefore obedience to the Civil Law is also part of the Law of Nature' (HL, 202,81–82,314, emphases added). Hobbes even says (exaggerating somewhat), that there is 'no obligation on any man, which ariseth not from some act of his own', hence our political obligations and liberties depend on 'what rights we pass away, when we make a commonwealth' (HL, 268).[14] It is very clear that, to Hobbes, these obligations depend not only on the advantages of political society, but also on our having performed one specific 'act of our own', the social contract.

Locke

The Restoration of King Charles II in 1660 did not end the political turbulence of seventeenth century Britain. In the 1680s a new struggle broke out against Charles's brother and successor James II, culminating in the latter's fall in 1688. In this successful fight against royal power a new political party was born – the Whigs, as they came to be called. The struggle also gave rise to a new theory of social contract, probably the most influential of all prior to Rousseau – that of John Locke. These two developments – the rise of the Whigs and the Lockean theory of social contract – were closely connected. Locke was from 1667 a close associate and leading adviser to Lord Ashley, later Earl of Shaftesbury, a prominent Whig politician and proponent of the 'exclusion' of James from the succession. Shaftesbury died in the Netherlands in 1683 after fleeing a charge of treason, and in the same year Locke too felt constrained to flee to the same destination, returning to England only in 1689, after the 'Glorious Revolution'. Locke's party was now in power, and before his death in 1704 he occupied a number of posts in government.

In the political struggles of the 1680s, the religious issue, so central in the Civil War, had by no means disappeared – King James himself was a Roman Catholic in a Protestant country – but it was subordinate to the constitutional issue of the relative authority of king and Parliament. The Whigs were, first and foremost, opponents of royal absolutism. Locke's social contract theory, accordingly, is an anti-absolutist theory and a justification of resistance to tyrants. Thus Locke's contract theory represents a return, after the magnificent aberration of Hobbes, to the characteristic political tendency of the social contract tradition, and in this sense resembles the contract theories of the Middle Ages, Renaissance and Reformation. In style of argument, however, it is quite unlike the medieval theories. Locke never refers to any contract between people and ruler, but instead relies on the individualist premises used to varying degrees by Salamonio and Althusius, and rigorously systematised by Hobbes. Naturally enough, indeed, the theory of Hobbes forms the inescapable background to Locke's argument, and – although Locke's major political work, the *Second Treatise of Government*, never mentions his great predecessor by name – several passages in it read like direct refutation of him. Locke's theory, then, combines some characteristically medieval attitudes to political power with a conceptual apparatus in many ways similar to that of Hobbes and the seventeenth century in general. But it is also significantly innovative, being the first contract theory to limit political authority through the idea of inalienable natural rights. This highly individualist conception was, perhaps, Locke's most significant bequest to the eighteenth and later centuries.

Central to Locke's argument, as to Hobbes's, is the contrast between the state of nature and civil (that is, political) society – the commonwealth, or as Locke even calls it in one place, 'the mighty Leviathan' (L, 50). In Locke's case there is no room for doubt that he believed the state of nature to be a historical phase – however brief – prior to government (L, 9,51–2 and *passim*). That apart, his account of the contrast gives every appearance of aiming to correct Hobbes's version. Locke thus denies that the state of nature is a state of war. What defines the state of nature, he says, is that men live together without a 'common judge with authority' over them; but this state is (or at least should be) a state of 'peace, good will, mutual assistance and preservation'. Yet Locke admits that, given the lack of a common judge, 'the state of war once begun continues' and that escaping from 'this state of war ... is one great reason of men's putting themselves into society and quitting the state of nature' (L, 11–12). Locke has here attempted an impossible amalgam of the Hobbesian account with a contrary stoic-derived 'golden age' conception of the state of nature – the latter being quite unsuited to a contract theory of government. In the end, therefore, he has not succeeded in disagreeing with Hobbes on this point.

Nevertheless, significant and genuine disagreements remain. Whereas in the Hobbesian version what distinguishes the state of nature from civil society is the absence of a common *power*, for Locke it is the absence of a common *judge*. This entails further differences. That there should be a need for judges implies that there is a law for them to adjudicate, already in the state of nature. For Locke, war in the state of nature arises out of breach of law – the law of nature. To Locke, this law of nature is a moral law in the full sense, known by reason, universally binding and (in contrast with Hobbes) fully operative in the state of nature. It arises from the mutual recognition of all men that they are equally

God's creatures and servants: hence, 'no one ought to harm another in his life, health, liberty or possessions'. Men are bound to respect this law; otherwise, they are perfectly free, in the state of nature, 'to order their actions and dispose of their possessions and persons as they think fit' (L, 4–5).

Thus for Locke as for Hobbes all men have a natural right of freedom, but Locke's natural right is much more restricted than Hobbes's. It is thus, unlike Hobbes's, no threat to peace, but is a concomitant of the moral law. Hence there is no reason to give it up. And being limited, the Lockean natural right of freedom can co-exist with *other* natural rights – for example the right to life and the right to possessions (or estate). Hence the famous Lockean trinity of natural rights – life, liberty and estate, sometimes referred to collectively as property, though this term is also used by Locke in the more conventional sense of a right to possessions only. Locke's theory of the natural right of property (in the narrow sense) is perhaps the most famous and controversial aspect of his entire political philosophy. There is no space here for a full account of it, but it should be noted that Locke upholds the right of a man to possess whatever he acquires by work, exchange, contract or bequest, and specifically defends the resulting 'inequality of private possessions' (L, 43,15–26,36,92). But this applies to the state of nature; in civil society the rights of individual property are not quite sacrosanct, as we shall see.

Locke's state of nature, then, is equipped with an extensive set of natural laws and natural rights which, if they were sufficiently respected, would ensure a peaceful and just society. The need for government – civil society – arises because they are not sufficiently respected. Breaches in the law of nature mean that the law must be enforced by suitable punishments, which in turn implies the necessity to judge that a breach has been committed. In the absence of political authority, says Locke, every man has the right to 'judge of and punish' breaches in the law of nature for himself. But *this* right is scarcely conducive to the maintenance of peace: many men are ignorant of the true law and biased in their interpretation and application of it, and in any case sufficient power to enforce correct punishments is often lacking. Hence *this* right – the 'executive power of the law of nature' – is the one that men must give up, and by giving up enter political society (L, 5–6,42f.,64–5). Must give up, that is, if they are to achieve peace and justice – for Locke, unlike Hobbes, does not claim that men are under any obligation to transfer any rights to the political community. He simply assumes that they have good reason to do so, and have done so in the overwhelming majority of cases – and that this is the origin of legitimate government, and the source of the individual's obligation to obey political authority. As Locke says, all men are by nature free and independent 'till, *by their own consents*, they make themselves members of some politic society' (L, 10).

Clearly, a political authority derived from such a limited transfer of individual rights must itself be strictly limited. To Locke, political authority is essentially authority to enforce the law of nature, and little more – or otherwise put, to defend the natural rights of individuals and the public good. This entails that it have the necessary executive power, and also provide an impartial system of adjudication to settle conflicts and disputes. But it further requires a legislature, to define clearly the (previously disputed) laws, and this legislative power, says Locke, is the supreme power in the commonwealth – supreme, but *not* unlimited. The disposition of the legislative power is therefore a crucial matter and one, says Locke, to be determined by the majority of the political community when first incorporated – they may establish a democracy, an oligarchy, a monarchy, or any mixture thereof. This establishment of legislators, and indeed rulers and magistrates generally is, says Locke (employing an ancient concept), a trust – they have been entrusted with power to defend the rights and welfare of their subjects (L, 44,65–9,75).

Locke's views on the limits of political authority and on the constitution of the legislative power together provide him with a theory of resistance to government. As we have seen, Locke has no objection to monarchical government but he is implacably hostile to *absolute* monarchy. Some of the most effective passages in his *Second Treatise* are those that attack Hobbes-like arguments for absolutism. 'Absolute monarchs are but men', Locke reminds us, and great as are the inconveniences of the state of nature due to men's being judges in their own case, yet they would have done better to remain in that state than, when quitting it, to agree

'that all of them but one should be under the restraint of laws, but that he should still retain all the liberty of the state of nature, increased with power, and made licentious by impunity. This is to think that men are so foolish that they take care to avoid what mischiefs may be done them by polecats or foxes, but are content, nay think it safely, to be devoured by lions.'

This is a deservedly famous piece of rhetoric. But Locke has a subtler and no less effective argument: absolute monarchy is actually *inconsistent* with civil society, for the absolute ruler remains judge in his own case – between him and his subjects there is no common, impartial judge, and a common impartial judge is precisely the institution that distinguishes civil society from the state of nature (L, 9,47,45).

The claim of rulers to absolute authority is an extreme case of what Locke calls tyranny (a concept for which Hobbes had no place), defined as 'the exercise of power beyond right'. Invasion of subjects' rights is a breach of the ruler's trust, and is one way in which, as Locke puts it, 'governments are dissolved' – that is, forfeit their legitimacy and their just claim to obedience. Such cases, Locke thinks, have been frequent in history, for the first governments to be established were probably monarchies which tended, in the course of time, to degenerate into tyrannies and thereby dissolve themselves. In such a case authority reverts to the members of the civil society as a whole, who may reallocate the powers of government as they see fit. In fact, Locke claims that peoples have generally come to see the wisdom of placing the legislative power in 'collective bodies of men, call them senate, parliament or what you please', so as to ensure that no individual is above the law (L, 100,109,55–8,73–5). Locke is thus a republican in the classic sense, though this does not preclude a monarchical *executive* bound by law – nor does Locke maintain that there is only one legitimate form of government. This is a matter for the people to decide when constituting their polity, or reconstituting it after dissolution.

But while the people may on due occasion re-constitute their government, any attempt by rulers to do so, is illegitimate, and counts as a further way in which a government is 'dissolved' and loses its authority. The legislative authority is 'sacred and unalterable in the hands where the community have once placed it'. The last chapter of Locke's *Second Treatise* contains a lengthy list of ways in which a 'prince' may illegitimately alter – in effect usurp – the legislative power, all having an obvious reference to strategies pursued by King James II in his struggle with his Parliamentary enemies. Clearly Locke thus intends to denounce the king, even though there is not the slightest reason to think that the constitution that he allegedly infringed had ever been established by a majority decision of the people. The chapter also refers to dissolution of government through the ruler's breach of trust, that is, his invasion of the rights of the people, and overall is clearly a general bill of indictment designed to justify resistance to King James (L, 106f.).

Thus it is in terms of breach of trust, not breach of contract, that Locke justifies resistance to government. As with Hobbes, rulers are not party to the original contract but (in contrast to Hobbes) that contract provides for the constituting of a government entrusted to act within certain specific limits. But breach of trust is a quasi-legal concept and therefore, Locke is aware, raises a problem of adjudication: 'Tis like, the common question will be made: Who shall be judge whether the prince or legislative act contrary to their trust?' Locke's answer is – whether the aggrieved party is a 'single man' or 'some of the people' – that 'the proper umpire in such a case should be the body of the people'. The people should be judge. But Locke suggests no mechanism by which the people could exercise this judicial function; rather, he suggests that, where such adjudication is impossible, or is made impossible by the intransigence of rulers, 'God in heaven is judge', and those who consider themselves the victims of tyranny 'have a liberty to appeal to heaven' – in other words, to resort to armed resistance, a kind of trial by battle (L, 121,85,122).

In brief summary, Locke's contract theory is a justification of the right to resist political authority in the name of individual rights to life, liberty and property, and in view of the great stress put by Locke on property rights, it is easy to see him as, in essence, the philosophical spokesman of the great Whig landowners who opposed and ultimately overthrew James II, and with whom Locke was himself so closely associated. A little more broadly, he can be seen as the spokesman of the property-owning classes (some commentators of Marxist persuasion even view him – somewhat anachronistically – as the spokesman of the rising bourgeoisie).[15] This interpretation is by no means without foundation. But here an important distinction is necessary: a distinction (which an influential school of scholars seem to wish to deny)[16] between Locke's intentions and his argument. Very likely, Locke intended by his theory to support a particular political party and an associated social class or stratum; but the fact remains that the essence of his argument is expressed in *universal* terms, in terms of natural rights of all human beings, and it extends to every single subject of political authority. Unlike so many of his contractarian predecessors, Locke never limited the right of resistance to political magnates supposed to be the natural 'representatives' of the people.

Something more needs to be said on the role of property in Locke's theory. Locke's preoccupation with property rights has this advantage, that it enables him to be (apparently) the first contract theorist to give an adequate account of the state as a *territorial* entity. The early contract theorists were less concerned with the state as such than with the personal relationship of rulers and ruled; and while Althusius portrayed the commonwealth as resulting from a merger of provinces and cities, his theory seems to give no hint of how these territorial units could result from the coalescence of private associations lacking any territorial jurisdiction. Locke's individualistic contract theory with its natural right of property makes the territory of the state in effect an amalgamation of land already owned by the contractors (L, 61–2). It is to be noted, too, that the contract somewhat modifies the pre-existing natural property right. For, as Locke acknowledges, government cannot be carried on without financial resources, and 'tis fit every one who enjoys his share of the protection should pay out of his estate his proportion for the maintenance of it'. How to reconcile this truth with the inalienable natural right to property? Locke's answer is that the necessary taxation of the subject 'must be with his own consent, i.e. the consent of the majority, giving it either by themselves or their representatives chosen by them' (L, 72–3). Locke sees a representative assembly as a much more stringent requirement for tax-raising purposes than for legislation.

Nevertheless, Locke's rapid equation of 'his own consent' with the consent of a majority of representatives has raised not a few critical eyebrows. And it is not only in relation to taxation that Locke's handling of his principle of consent gives rise to problems. For consent is at the heart of Locke's theory of legitimate political authority. 'No one can be ... subjected to the political power of another, without his own consent' (L, 49). And Locke means *free* consent, not (by contrast with Hobbes) submission to power such as that of a conqueror (L, chapter XVI). This free consent was given, Locke believes, through the original contract, made in a state of nature. But what of later generations born under government? For Locke, they cannot be bound by the consent of their ancestors or anyone else, but are completely at liberty when they come of age, to decide whether or not to put themselves under any government. How, in practice do they do so? Unfortunately it is not possible to give a coherent account of Locke's view on this important matter. On the one hand, there is his famous (or notorious) doctrine of 'tacit consent': that is, 'any man who hath any possessions, or enjoyment of any part of the dominions of any government', including therein 'the very being of any one under the territories of that government', thereby gives his tacit consent to its authority; and Locke also tells us that by taking up an inheritance of his father's property, a son voluntarily puts himself under 'the government ... there established', this being an understood condition of the inheritance of property, which government protects. Also, the same applies to all ownership of land, which indeed is part of the territory of the commonwealth: acquiring such land is therefore the giving of tacit consent. On the other hand, Locke also affirms that tacit consent does not make a man a *member* of a political society – only 'his actually entering into it by positive engagement, and *express* promise and compact' does so. Yet the inheritance of property by heirs, Locke also says, makes the latter *members* of political society (L, 60–3). One well-known interpretation of all this, is that Locke, here once again, is surreptitiously proposing the rule of property-owners (or even capitalists) over the rest of the population (cf. Macpherson, 1962). In fact, however, Locke's statements are so contradictory that no consistent interpretation is possible. The best that can be said for Locke here is that he appears to be at least trying to mark the important distinction between mere subjection to authority (in return for protection of rights), and active membership in a political society or commonwealth; important, not least, because of the role that Locke's theory occasionally assigns to the 'people'. But it can hardly be said that he succeeded.

These confusions aside, Locke's extension of the concept of consent to include 'the very being of any one within the territories' of a government has attracted much criticism. If consent is understood as broadly as this, is there any way in which a person could withhold his consent? Is Locke really allowing individuals any freedom of choice in the matter, after all? The answer is that, for Locke, there is only one way to refuse consent to an established government's authority and that is, to keep out of its territory, or if in it, to leave it (L, 61–2). In taking this view, Locke has a famous and ancient forerunner – Socrates, as reported by his pupil Plato in the *Crito*. Socrates, in a famous speech, endorses this principle:

> 'that any Athenian, on attaining to manhood and seeing for himself the political organization of the State and . . . its Laws, is permitted, if he is not satisfied . . . to go away wherever he likes . . . On the other hand, if any one [stays], we hold that by so doing he has in fact undertaken to do anything [the Laws] tell him; and we maintain that anyone who disobeys is guilty of doing wrong.' (Plato 1959, p.92)

Locke may have been familiar with this passage, and even influenced by it, but it should be noticed that he would not have endorsed its conclusion. Consent, for Locke, is not a sufficient condition of political obligation, though it is a necessary one. In addition, governments are, as we have seen, bound by natural law and, if they violate it, may be forcibly resisted.

Patriarchalism and social contract theory

As stated in our introductory chapter, one major rival of contractarian theory in its seventeenth century heyday was the conception of government known as patriarchalism, which (briefly put) identified paternal and political authority. Naturally, therefore, the contract theorists too had to give some attention to the nature of authority in the family and its relation to that in civil society; and so must we.

As expressed in its canonical form by the royalist Sir Robert Filmer, patriarchalism may be briefly summarised.[17] Adam, the father of the human race, was given by God not merely fatherly but (what was the same thing) absolute monarchical power over his offspring. All political authority is of this kind. All human beings are descendants of Adam, and all legitimate rulers are (or are 'reputed' to be) his heirs, and have inherited his powers. All subjects therefore owe absolute obedience to legitimate kings. From this it follows that all talk of a 'state of nature' in the sense of a pre-political condition of mankind, is absurd; men have been subject to political authority from their first creation. Equally absurd is talk of men's natural freedom and equality; men have from the first been placed by God under monarchical government, and absolute government at that.

Clearly this extreme, biblicist form is not the only one that patriarchalism could take – one could also arrive at it, for example, by combining Aristotle's view that familial authority is essentially monarchical, with a denial or ignoring of his distinction between the familial and political realms. Filmer, indeed, did not fail to cite Aristotle as an authority, even though a much less prominent one than the Bible. In any case, it was to Filmer's version of patriarchalism that Locke specifically addressed himself, especially in the lengthy refutation contained in the *First Treatise of Government*. In the *Second Treatise* also, the subject is again taken up in chapter VI ('Of Paternal Power') and chapter XV ('Of Paternal, Political and Despotical Power Considered Together'). Here Locke, as might be expected, stresses the *difference* between the power of parents (not only fathers, Locke remarks) and that of civil rulers. The legitimate power of parents over offspring derives from the dependency of the latter, and their need for protection; when this ceases, so too does legitimate parental power. In a famous phrase, Locke remarks that 'we are born free, as we are born rational', meaning by this that we are born to *become* both: on reaching due age, the individual is free of parental tutelage, and free to consent (or not consent) to political authority. Locke readily admits that, in all likelihood, many of the earliest political rulers were fathers or patriarchs of large extended family groupings; but he stresses that the legitimacy of *this* rule rested 'not [on] any paternal right, but only [on] the *consent* of his children' – a consent that it was, after all, natural enough to give at first, even if subsequent experience was to cast doubt on the wisdom of monarchical rule, and to lead to its reconstitution (L, 29,31,37–9).

It is interesting to compare Locke's response to patriarchalism with that of Hobbes. Hobbes rejected patriarchalist premises in a more thorough-going way – not so much by contrasting family and commonwealth, as by rejecting the patriarchalist account, not just of the commonwealth, but also of the family itself. *Natural* dominion over a child, Hobbes asserts, belongs not to the father, but to the mother, 'seeing the infant is first in the power of the mother', and in any case 'it cannot be known who is the father, unless it be declared by the mother'. *Paternal* power, therefore, derives not from 'generation', but from consent: both the consent of the mother, in an agreement with the father, *and* the consent of the child, 'either express, or by other sufficient arguments declared'. Thus the family, like the state, is a contractual, not a natural association, though the kind of state to which Hobbes compares it is 'that which some writers call despotical', that is, one based on conquest, in which the ruled recognise the logic of superior power. Such families thus governed by legitimate 'despotic' fathers, existed in the state of nature, and indeed, Hobbes says, 'for the most part Commonwealths have been erected by the fathers ... of families', rather than by totally isolated individuals (HL, 253–5). This contrasts with Locke's picture of commonwealths emerging by *extension and modification* of (qualitatively different) family government. In a formal sense, Hobbes's account is more similar to Althusius's view of the genetic relationship between family and commonwealth, even though, politically speaking, Locke and Althusius are much closer together than either is to Hobbes.

5 Culmination, Critique and Restatement of Contract Theory

Our task in this chapter is to depict the culmination of the classic phase of contract theory, and at the same time the development of a powerful critique of its basic postulates. This critique did not by any means immediately destroy the currency of the theory – that was the work of the late eighteenth and early nineteenth centuries. Nevertheless, the contract theorists whose work we shall now survey differ in an important respect from almost all the major figures we have previously discussed. Manegold, Engelbert, Salamonio, Duplessis-Mornay, Althusius, Hobbes and Locke, no matter how 'scholarly' or 'theoretical' or 'practical' or 'polemical' they may have been in style and approach, were each and every one intimately concerned with (if not actually involved in) major political struggles and problems of their time, and produced their contract theories in this context. This is *not* to say that they are relevant only to such a limited context; it is to say that these universal theories were stimulated and informed by this particular kind of political experience.

Of the important contract theorists to be discussed in this chapter – Pufendorf, Rousseau, Kant – this no longer holds true. The contributions of Pufendorf and Kant are essentially academic, with no obvious relation to, or genesis in, important political struggles of the time. This may be viewed as either gain or loss – as a loss or urgency and immediate political relevance, or a gain in terms of disinterested pursuit of truth. As for Rousseau, while he was by temperament and position no academic, and the *Social Contract* rapidly became embroiled (and embroiled its author) in political conflicts in his native Geneva, still the main stimulus of his theories was not so much any political crisis, as his response to his own experience of contemporary European society, and his concern with the moral predicament of the individual. But – it need scarcely be said – the relatively limited role of contemporary politics in the genesis of these contract theories is a completely different matter from their political *influence*, which was often considerable, and in the case of Rousseau, enormous.

Contract theory in seventeenth-century Europe

The previous chapter presented the growth of contract theory in the seventeenth century almost wholly in British terms. Needless to say, however, contract theories did not cease to be produced elsewhere in Europe in this period. One such theory is that of the Dutchman Spinoza, but with this we may deal very briefly. For Spinoza's theory, though quite widely admired, is a strange one indeed. Politically speaking, his most passionate concern, it seems, was to defend religious freedom. Yet his theory outdoes Hobbes in deriving totally absolute sovereign authority from totally egoistic human nature, combining both with an unmitigated determinism and a corresponding denial of all moral obligation.[1] Never, perhaps, has there been a theory less adapted to support its author's political views.

Spinoza's German contemporary, Samuel Pufendorf (both were born in 1632) requires lengthier consideration, not least because of the immense authority his theories acquired. Pufendorf's major treatise (*De Jure Naturae et Gentium*)[2] impresses by its sheer scale, its enormous scope and impressive systematisation. In the eighteenth century it became a standard text and a powerful intellectual influence, especially but by no means only in Germany. Among many others, it certainly influenced Locke (though more as to premises than conclusions).

In brief summary, Pufendorf's project may be described as follows: to endorse the political conclusions of Hobbes, but to divorce them from Hobbes's more shocking and scandalous arguments, to soften the bluntness with which he had stated them and to correct Hobbes's errors. In many respects the basic concepts and assumptions of Pufendorf's arguments are similar to those of Hobbes; he agrees that in the pre-political state of nature, where men had 'no common master', human selfishness and aggression were such as to produce 'the rule of passion, war, fear, poverty, ugliness, ... ignorance and savagery'. Yet Hobbes was wrong to suppose that in this state there was no justice or injustice, no binding moral law. On the contrary, since man is on his own a helpless and vulnerable creature, dependent on the mutual assistance of his fellows, 'it follows that ... he must be sociable'. The 'laws of this sociability', which teach how to be 'a good member of human society' are, Pufendorf says, natural laws. These laws enjoin, among other things, the keeping of promises and agreements. And, Pufendorf adds, here anticipating many a modern critic of Hobbes, if the obligation to keep agreements did not *precede* the establishment of government, how could there be any obligation to obey rulers established by compact? What would 'prevent subjects from throwing off obedience and destroying the state at their pleasure? ... For it would be idle to hope that so great a multitude of men could hold together by the force of mere violence and fear' (POH, 89,91,18–19,48; PJN, 1139).

Pufendorf is much more orthodox than Hobbes, not only in his moral, but also in his religious views. According to Pufendorf, the war-like state of nature was not man's first condition; he agrees with Filmer that the first men were subject to the paternal authority of Adam. Later, they and their descendants 'left the paternal homes' and 'nearly every male set up a household for himself'. This collection of patriarchically governed households constitutes, for Pufendorf, the state of nature, with all its defects, requiring civil government as the remedy. Pufendorf is much more explicit than Hobbes (for whom the point was something of an afterthought) that the formation of the state was the work of patriarchs, already exercising authority over households, and empowered to commit their dependents to accept political authority (POH, 90,97,101).

Pufendorf again takes issue with Hobbes as to the way in which this political authority was constituted. Hobbes was wrong to suppose, Pufendorf thinks, that men would have agreed with one another on a total renunciation of their natural liberty to a sovereign, without receiving from him any reciprocal promise of protection (PJN, 977–80). To correct Hobbes, Pufendorf reverts to a version of the contract which is formally rather similar to that of Althusius. The establishment of a state requires two compacts:

in the first, men agree to enter a 'permanent community' of 'fellow-citizens', that is, they pledge themselves to accept political authority. This first pact must also provide for the taking of a decision (Pufendorf calls it a decree) by the political community, as to how, and by whom, they will be ruled. The second pact is between these rulers, and the rest of the political community: the former 'bind themselves to take care of the common security and safety, the rest to yield them their obedience'. As for later generations of subjects, Pufendorf says, in language that seems to anticipate Locke, that they become so 'by a tacit pact'. But while the language may sound Lockean, the substance is more Hobbesian. Since 'those who establish states in the first place are surely not held to have done so with the thought that they would cease with the death of their founders . . . , all who are born in a state are also understood to have subjected themselves to that sovereignty' (POH, 104–7; PJN, 994). They have, in other words, no real choice.

Nevertheless, Pufendorf's version of social contract theory seems to put subjects in a relatively strong moral position *vis-à-vis* their rulers, who are bound *both* by their contract with the people (as in Althusius and so many earlier theorists) *and* by natural law (as in Locke). Indeed, Pufendorf explicitly repudiates Hobbes on both these points, taking him to task for refusing 'to recognize any distinction between supreme and absolute sovereignty' (PJN, 1077,1103). Yet Pufendorf's quarrel with Hobbes is much more philosophical than political: he does not, in fact, wish to provide any justification for resistance. Even although theoretically bound by contract and natural law, the supreme political authority is, says Pufendorf, 'unaccountable, in other words, not bound so to render account to any human being that, if that person did not approve the account, it would for that reason be liable to human penalities or constraint'. If it were, it would not be supreme. (Presumably rulers are accountable only to God.) It follows that 'not only is it wrong to resist [the sovereign's] legitimate demands, but also the citizens must patiently bear with its severity . . . Even when it has threatened the most cruel injuries, individuals will seek their safety in flight or endure any amount of misfortune, rather than draw the sword' against their sovereign. The good citizen must 'have no thought of revolution' (POH, 116,144). In the end, therefore, Pufendorf's agreement with Hobbes about the horrors of the state of nature[3] outweighs all else: while repudiating absolutism, and urging rulers to seek the welfare of the people above all, (POH, 121–2), he at the same time inculcates a duty of passive obedience. His thought is thus much in harmony with that so-called 'enlightened despotism' that was to develop in Germany and elsewhere in the eighteenth century. Pufendorf – who himself served three monarchs at different stages of his highly successful career – may have done something to help it grow.

Rousseau

If the eighteenth century was the era of 'enlightened despotism' in continental Europe, that era came to a violent end in 1789, the year of the French Revolution. This event was not unrelated, perhaps, to the theory of social contract; at any rate, only a few decades previously the *ancien régime* of Europe had encountered a revolutionary intellectual challenge from the most famous of social contract theorists, Rousseau. Rousseau represents the culmination of the classic phase of contract theory; and while it would be a gross exaggeration of the power of ideas to describe the French Revolution as its practical culmination in European history, yet it would be an exaggeration containing a grain of truth.

Rousseau's views as to what constitutes good and bad government are extremely clear; his arguments on the subject are sometimes less so. So far as the theory of social contract is concerned, the question is complicated by the fact that he wrote on the subject not once, but twice. Before *The Social Contract* itself appeared (in 1762), Rousseau had already treated the subject in his *Discourse on the Origin of Inequality* (1755). The accounts of the contract given in these two works are quite different. Nevertheless, they are not necessarily contradictory. They can be reconciled by the supposition that, while the discussion in the 1755 *Discourse* is a more or less familiar kind of contract theory, concerned with the historical origin of government, what Rousseau offers in *The Social Contract* is a new brand of that theory, namely an *ideal* contract, still ostensibly concerned with the origin of government, but with how, ideally, it *ought* to have been established, rather than how it actually *was* established. Rousseau's views on what constitutes legitimate political authority stem from this latter, ideal contract, rather than from any actual contract: as he says in chapter 1 of *The Social Contract*, he is concerned in that book, not with how men lost their natural liberty, but with 'what can make it [the loss] legitimate' (R, 165). This marks a considerable departure in the history of contract theory, which had hitherto sought to derive the terms of legitimate rule from the contract or contracts by which civil society actually originated. Hence the original contract discussed in the *Discourse* is after all not so traditional – it does not have the normative significance for Rousseau that it had for earlier theorists.

It must be admitted that this interpretation of Rousseau's two texts encounters some difficulties. For example, in the passage of *The Social Contract* cited above, Rousseau says also that he does not *know* how men lost their natural liberty; and in the *Discourse* itself he says that his investigations 'must not be considered as historical truths, but only as mere conditional and hypothetical reasoning, rather calculated to explain the nature of things, than to ascertain their actual origin' (R, 45). It looks, perhaps, as if Rousseau never intended to offer a theory of the historical origin of government at all. However, the interpretation of this remark is not straightforward, as many commentators have pointed out. Its context is a reference to orthodox religion, which, as Rousseau says, 'commands us to believe that God Himself having taken men out of a state of nature immediately after the creation, they are unequal only because it is His will they should be so'. Since the whole of Rousseau's *Discourse* is an onslaught on human inequality, it is not possible that Rousseau himself believes what, he avows, religion commands us to believe. There were, however, very good reasons of prudence why he should not say so right out, and hence distance himself from his own account. That account is unquestionably in the form of a historical narrative. It is entirely reasonable for Rousseau to say that he does not *know* that it is true; it is, rather, as he elsewhere puts it, a 'hypothetical history of governments', (R, 43), that is, a schematic account of what, given the available evidence, Rousseau thinks most likely to have happened.

Even if we adopt this interpretation of Rousseau's two texts, we need to notice a difference between them in relation to the important concept of the state of nature. In both texts, Rousseau uses the term to refer to man's most primitive condition. In *The*

Social Contract this is contrasted simply with man's political state, more or less as in Hobbes and Locke. In the *Discourse* of 1755, however, Rousseau outlines a quite elaborate sequence of events, by which men passed from a primitive, unsocial condition, to society, and then to government; and here, the natural state is contrasted, not only with the political state, but with the social state also. It should be stressed that there is no inconsistency if one text describes the actual while the other prescribes the ideal. We shall thus henceforth consider Rousseau's two texts as providing a single composite theory of the human condition in its relation to government and politics.

We can start from a point on which the two texts explicitly agree with each other, and with a long line of social contract theorists, that in the state of nature men were free and equal – no man has, by nature, any legitimate authority over any other (R, 39,166,169). The *Discourse* of 1755, as its full title indicates, is an account of how this primitive natural equality of men came to be destroyed. But it is no mere neutral account, but rather a passionate indictment of actual inequality. The growth of inequality is for Rousseau at the same time the growth of human corruption, and Rousseau's denunciation of both is an expression of his revulsion against eighteenth century European society as he knew it. This is the point of view from which he considers the question of government.

Rousseau's view of human history as a history of moral degeneration enables him at once to contradict the account of human nature given by writers such as Hobbes (though Hobbes is not attacked by name until later): writers who, 'constantly dwelling on wants, avidity, oppression, desires and pride [have] transferred to the state of nature ideas which were acquired in society; so that, in speaking of the savage, they described the social man' (R, 45,65). Hobbes, Rousseau implies, has read into the nature of man features of his character which are actually the result of a long process of social corruption.

For the earliest men, according to Rousseau, being not social creatures at all, could scarcely have the vices attributed by Hobbes to human nature. They wandered 'up and down the forests, without industry, without speech, and without homes' – 'the same persons hardly met twice in their lives'. They knew nothing of marriage, family or property, or any other social institution. They had no mutual 'moral relations or determinate obligations', hence 'could not be either good or bad, virtuous or vicious' (R, 72,58,64,69). In brief, they were, or appeared, little different from other animals. Rousseau grants to Hobbes that natural men were actuated by self-interest, and may occasionally have quarrelled; but without 'very bloody consequences', for their natural self-love was mitigated by an equally natural compassion for their fellows. Above all, natural man had yet to develop the vice of *amour propre* (Rousseau's term, roughly, for what Hobbes called 'glory'), that is, the desire for superiority over others, which is a product of society. He thus, says Rousseau, acted in accord with the maxim, 'Do good to yourself with as little evil as possible to others', and as a result the state of nature, contrary to Hobbes, was 'the best calculated to promote peace' among men (R, 66,69,68,65).

Yet men are, of course, not as other animals. What distinguishes human nature from the rest is a potentiality, what Rousseau calls 'perfectibility' (R, 54) – possibly with some irony. Human beings can, and have, transformed the conditions of their own lives; in brief, they have learned. Among other things, they learned the advantages of social co-operation; and after 'a multitude of ages' came the 'first revolution' of human history, which established families, and, in the form of simple dwelling-places, rudimentary property. Collections of settled families formed simple communities. 'This period', opines Rousseau, 'must have been the happiest and most stable of epochs ... and altogether the very best man could experience'. It also allowed notable technical and economic progress to occur. Yet this first revolution was far from pure gain, even if its dangers were not at once apparent. The increased goods made available by material progress would become a 'yoke' – in course of time they lost 'almost all their power to please, and even degenerated into real needs, till the want of them became far more disagreeable than the possession of them had been pleasant'. They became, in a word, corrupting. So did another concomitant of early society.

'Each person began to consider the rest and to wish to be considered in turn; and thus a value began to be attached to public esteem. Whoever danced best, whoever was the handsomest, the strongest, the most dexterous, or the most eloquent, came to be of most consideration; and this was the first step towards inequality, and at the same time towards vice.

From the first distinctions arose on the one side vanity and contempt and on the other shame and envy.'

In other words, *amour propre* was born: the march of civilization and corruption would begin, and end by being 'fatal to innocence and happiness' (R, 79,82–3,80,81). A second 'great revolution' accelerated the process – the development of settled agriculture. One concomitant of such cultivation was private property in land; another was division of labour, since it called for specialised production of metal tools; a third was trade; and the upshot of all these was a huge development of inequality, economic and social, among men. This diagnosis does not in fact contradict Locke; but Rousseau differs vastly from Locke in his evaluation of the whole process. To Rousseau, it is a process of moral corruption, in which men became one another's enemies, vainglorious, ambitious, the rich 'imperious and cruel' to the poor, the poor 'sly and artful' towards the rich. 'Usurpations by the rich, robbery by the poor, and the unbridled passions of both ... filled men with avarice, ambition and vice ... There arose perpetual conflicts, which never ended but in battles and bloodshed. The new-born state of society thus gave rise to a horrible state of war' (R, 83–6,87–8). This was the state of affairs that Hobbes mistook for the state of nature.

From this point on, Rousseau's theory of government in the 1755 *Discourse* is, up to a point, traditional. The 'horrible state of war' made government necessary. But this is not, for Rousseau, the whole story. Not everyone had equal need of government; the principal sufferers from the state of war were the rich, those with property to lose. It was therefore the rich who took the initiative in introducing government; and while, indeed, government was the outcome of a general agreement, that agreement was achieved only by cunning on the part of the rich.

'[The rich man] readily devised plausible arguments to make [the poor] close with his design. "Let us join", said he, "to guard the weak from oppression, to restrain the ambitious, and secure to every man the possession of what belongs to him ... let us collect [our forces] in a supreme power which may govern us by wise laws, protect and defend all the members of the association, repulse their common enemies, and maintain eternal harmony among us".'

The result, Rousseau suggests, was that 'All ran headlong to their chains, in hopes of securing their liberty; for they had just wit enough to perceive the advantages of political institutions, without experience enough to enable them to foresee the dangers . . .' This event 'bound new fetters on the poor, and gave new powers to the rich, irretrievably destroyed natural liberty, eternally fixed the law of property and inequality . . . and subjected [almost] all mankind to perpetual labour, slavery and wretchedness' (R, 88,89).

Here we have Rousseau's revolutionary version of the original contract of government – portrayed as the outcome of cunning and short-sightedness, and having as its result the stabilisation of inequality and oppression. Such a contract, one might suppose, could provide no basis for the legitimation of government, for it could have no legitimacy itself. Rather, it appears to portray the governments known to human history as mechanisms for institutionalising the rule of the rich over the poor (a view which prefigures that of Karl Marx). And such is, indeed, Rousseau's view of the governments of men. However, it is not quite true to say that for Rousseau the original contract has no validity. On this he is equivocal; and the reason seems to be that, in the 1755 *Discourse*, he pursues two imperfectly integrated themes. One is his account of, and onslaught on, inequality, from which point of view government appears in a largely negative light. But Rousseau was also influenced by more traditional contractarian thinking, which used the original contract as a way of setting limits to governmental authority. In this Lockean vein he writes that men first took to themselves 'superiors' only for the sake of 'protection for their lives, liberties and properties', not as absolute rulers. Such was the 'contract between the people and the chiefs chosen by them'. But the chiefs or rulers have been able, in the course of history, to circumvent its terms, and set themselves up as absolute hereditary kings (R, 92,96). Rousseau's combination of themes, in fact, enables him to attack the existing political regimes twice over: first by indicating the morally dubious nature of the original contract of government itself; second, by charging that, in addition, existing regimes anyway constitute a breach of its terms. *Both* the origin of government, *and* the subsequent aggrandisement of rulers, represent successive stages in the intensification of human inequality (R, 98–9).

Such, in Rousseau's eyes, has been the – largely disastrous – course of human history. How, though, *should* mankind have arranged its affairs? So far as politics is concerned, Rousseau's answer is given in the famous *Social Contract*. Unlike Marx, Rousseau does not reject the legitimacy of the state as such, but prescribes the conditions of the legitimate state – the terms, that is, of the legitimate social contract. In historical terms, this contract clearly ought to have been made *before* the development of social and economic inequality – which means, perhaps, before the development of society itself.[4] Rousseau remains, in *The Social Contract*, much concerned about equality. But a new concern is even more apparent – that of liberty. The problem of the social compact, Rousseau says, in a much quoted passage, 'is to find a form of association which will defend and protect with the whole common force the person and goods of each associate, and in which each, while uniting himself with all, may still obey himself alone, and remain as free as before'. And his solution to the problem is his celebrated (and perplexing) concept of the general will: each associate 'puts his person and all his power under the supreme direction of the general will'. Each associate would thus become a member of a collective body, capable of acting through an assembly of the associates, who would thus collectively exercise sovereign political authority, the right to make laws governing the state (R, 174,175,192).

Rousseau makes it clear that this sovereign political authority consisting of all citizens is both supreme and unlimited. It is an absolute sovereignty. The individual associates who are parties to the contract cannot retain any of their rights; if they did, Rousseau suggests, 'there would be no common superior to decide between them and the public, each being ... his own judge', and the state of nature would in effect continue (R, 174,176). It looks as if Rousseau is here trying to avoid the kind of resistance to authority, and consequent civil turbulence, that is legitimated by Locke's theory of natural rights. This is understandable, in view of the fact that the constitution prescribed by Rousseau in *The Social Contract* is that of an *ideal* state, where, it might be hoped, such resistance would have no place. But it remains questionable whether *any* constitution can be so ideal as to ensure this.

If Rousseau will not allow the individual citizen of his ideal state any inalienable natural rights, how then is his liberty – so prized by Rousseau – to be safeguarded? This is a vexed question indeed, which cannot be adequately discussed here. According to Rousseau, the ideal social contract constitutes an exchange of 'natural liberty' for 'civil liberty', and civil liberty means, essentially, rule by a sovereign body in which each citizen has an equal share, and which thus expresses the 'general will' (R, 178). This latter definition of liberty is not as eccentric as it may seem – the notion of a 'free constitution', current in the eighteenth and even the nineteenth century and stemming from classical times (in the literature of which Rousseau was himself steeped), meant, more or less, simply a non-monarchical state governed according to law. In terms of Benjamin Constant's famous contrast, Rousseau suggests that men, by the ideal social contract, exchange the 'liberty of the moderns' for the 'liberty of the ancients'. But it must be admitted that the similarity of terminology masks a great difference in meaning.

Rousseau tries to narrow the gap through his concept of the general will.[5] While his discussion of the whole matter is far from lucid, it appears that he thinks that, if the sovereign law-making body consists of all citizens equally, and makes laws that apply to all citizens equally, it is likely to respect and further their common interests, that is the interests that all equally share, and in this sense to embody the will of each citizen as a citizen (though not necessarily his will in so far as it is not general, that is, represents interests not shared by all citizens). Thus Rousseau feels able to claim that enforcing laws made by such a sovereign is (in a famous or notorious phrase) forcing the individual 'to be free' (R, 176–7, 185,187–8). Yet Rousseau is clear that such laws are to be made by majority decision, not unanimity (R, 250), and in fact never succeeds (despite valiant attempts) in showing how a tyranny of the majority (invested, in effect, with absolute sovereignty) could be definitely excluded. Probably, in fact, no constitutional design, however ideal, can guarantee to exclude tyranny, and it therefore follows that any political theorist concerned to prevent tyranny – as Rousseau certainly was – must, like Locke, allow an ultimate right of resistance, however unpalatable this conclusion may be.

A noteworthy feature of Rousseau's theory is that it shows him to be unique among the many social contract theorists who have postulated man's liberty and equality in a state of nature in that he wishes to preserve both their liberty *and* their equality in the civil state. His ideal constitution does indeed preserve this equality, thus making Rousseau the great exponent of what may be called the 'democratic' social contract (though he himself uses the term 'democracy' in a different sense) (R, 216–18). But his attempt to safeguard liberty seems to be a failure. Indeed, he seems at times to confuse the two *desiderata* – to suppose that, if equality is safeguarded, liberty necessarily will be too. Rousseau seems to think that the contrary of freedom is 'personal dependence' – dependence on a master, a condition that Rousseau had himself known all too directly as a young apprentice in Geneva, and which of course negates freedom and equality at the same time. In a sovereign republic of equals, no one is dependent on a master (there are no superiors and inferiors as Rousseau points out (R, 174,177)) – but he does not adequately cope with the possibility that the individual may still be oppressed by the sovereign body operating by majority vote.

We may add a final word by way of comparison between the actual contract envisaged by Rousseau in the *Discourse on the Origin of Inequality*, and the ideal contract depicted in *The Social Contract*. The former is, in Gierke's terminology, a contract of rulership, agreed between the people and their 'chiefs', setting the conditions of government; the latter, though it establishes political authority, is a contract between individuals in a state of nature. According to Rousseau, the ideal contract establishes a sovereign, not a government; for him, a government is a subordinate element of the constitution, charged with executing the sovereign's will. Rousseau is not greatly concerned whether government, in this sense, is monarchic, aristocratic, or democratic: what he insists on is that magistrates 'are not the people's masters, but its officers; [hence] it can set them up and pull them down whenever it likes'. The title of one of Rousseau's chapters proclaims 'that the institution of government is *not* a contract' – for magistrates 'there is no question of contract, but of obedience' (R, 208f.,245,242). The duty of princes, in other words, is to carry out the will of the sovereign people. Since Rousseau also wrote that 'we are obliged to obey only legitimate powers' (R, 168), implying that we may resist illegitimate ones, it is not hard to see why Rousseau's theory of government was to be so popular with the revolutionaries of 1789, and, even more, with those of 1792, the Jacobins.

Critics of social contract theory

Rousseau's theory of social contract is the climax of a centuries-long tradition of political thought. Long before he wrote, however, social contract theory had been the target of criticism, and soon afterwards the volume of criticism became so great as, apparently, to kill the theory off more or less totally, not to revive with any strength until recent times. We must now turn our attention to some of the objections to contract theory.

Any non-contractarian theory of political authority is perhaps implicitly a criticism of contract theory, but such theories are far too numerous to be surveyed here. Instead, we must confine ourselves to explicit attacks on contract theory itself. One of the earliest of such attacks seems to have come from a royal pen, that of James VI and I of Scotland and England, in his *True Law of Free Monarchy* of 1598 (ironically, James had been tutored in his youth by the contract theorist, George Buchanan). James not only claimed to be king by divine right, but also analysed what the contrary notion, that kingship arose from a contract, would entail; namely, James argued, a particular sort of constitution, in which breaches of the contract could be determined 'in a lawful trial ... by the ordinary judge'. Without provision for such lawful trial, the supposed contract cannot be brought to bear, unless 'every man may be both party and judge in his own case, which is absurd' (F, 93, cited). King James, of course, had particularly in mind potential rebels against royal power. He argues that the absence of the necessary judicial institutions shows the absurdity of justifying such resistance by a social contract, and, indeed, of the contract theory in general.

As a matter of fact, judicial institutions of the requisite sort have not been totally lacking in European history. In the medieval kingdom of Aragon there existed the office of the Justice, independent of the king, and empowered to arbitrate in certain circumstances between the king and his subjects. At least according to certain theorists, the Justice had been created, along with the king, at the institution of the Aragonese kingdom, precisely in order to uphold the original contract on which the kingdom was founded. These facts and theories were known to and invoked by the Huguenot opponents of the French monarchy, including Duplessis-Mornay. This particular theory of the origin of the Justice appears to be false; but of his existence, and occasionally important role, there is no doubt.[6]

Nevertheless, the argument levelled against contract theory by King James is a cogent one. The Justice of Aragon shows only that a judge of the contract is not impossible, and might even have existed in one case. But contract theory, as a *general* theory of government, needs to give a *general* answer to the question of adjudication. Nor, in fact, did contract theorists entirely fail to do so. As we saw above, Manegold of Lautenbach allotted the function of adjudicating the contract between king and people to the Pope; while the Calvinist contract theorists gave it to the 'lesser magistrates', those with a political calling.[7] For his part, Locke argued that the judge of whether a ruler had breached his trust should be 'the people', but without specifying any possible way in which it could exercise this role. So Locke's solution to the problem of adjudication is scarcely satisfactory, while those of the papalists and Calvinists seem too much like special pleading.

King James's argument was repeated (indeed, quoted) by a somewhat later English royalist, Sir Robert Filmer, who also added some further criticisms of contract theory on his own account. Filmer, as we have seen, held that kings have inherited the patriarchal powers of Adam; the contrary theory, that they derived their authority from the people (by contract or otherwise) is, Filmer charges, incoherent. In effect, Filmer's argument is that this theory cannot account for the actual multiplicity of states and kingdoms. If the establishment of political authority in a state of nature requires the agreement of 'the people', why does it not require the agreement of all the people of the world? How could it come about that 'particular multitudes' had authority to establish 'several commonwealths' each with its particular ruler or rulers (F, 81)?

To this a contract theorist could reply that any group would be entitled to establish an authority so long as the authority in question held sway only over the members of that group. But Filmer's argument does have some cogency in relation to the kind of contract theory that postulates only a contract between a people and its ruler, in that such a theory fails to explain how any particular 'people' was itself constituted. On the other hand, it appears to have no force against those contract theories that base political authority directly on the agreement of individuals (as in the case of Hobbes, Locke and Rousseau) or else derive membership in a political community, directly or indirectly, from such agreements (as in Althusius and Pufendorf).

Filmer has another argument against contract theory – the argument of the plain man of common sense against the philosopher. Quite simply, the notion that government originated in a contract – of whatever kind – is hopelessly unrealistic. Supposing distinct peoples to have been formed out of the state of nature, then, Filmer asks rhetorically, 'Was a general meeting of [a] whole kingdom ever known for the election of a Prince?', and answers his own question thus: 'To conceit such a thing is to image little less than an impossibility' (F, 81). Early contract theorists avoided this problem by postulating that the people contracted through their representatives (meaning thereby the great men of the kingdom, not their elected representatives). Understandably, Filmer will not accept this as legitimate. As for the notion of individuals covenanting with one another to lay down their natural right, not only would that be impossible on a world-wide scale, 'it is not possible to be done in the smallest kingdom, though all men should spend their whole lives in nothing else but in running up and down to covenant' (F, 243). Many later commentators have agreed with Filmer that the social contract theory of the origin of states is very poor history (though they have not been disposed to prefer Filmer's patriarchalist alternative).

We shall later have to consider how serious an objection to contract theory is this alleged lack of historical reality. It might possibly be retorted against Filmer that he interpreted the 'original contract' in an unduly literal way, precisely in order to make it seem ridiculous. At any rate, the next critic of contract theory to be considered, the Scottish philosopher David Hume, who is also one of the most penetrating of all, construed the idea more broadly than Filmer, and did not rest his case on its historical implausibility. On the contrary, Hume, in his famous essay 'Of the Original Contract', published in 1742, explicitly allowed that 'if we trace government to its first origin in the woods and deserts' it is undeniable that it was 'at first, founded on a contract'. By this he does not mean that men then subscribed to a 'compact or agreement ... expressly formed for general submission' – they were much too uncultivated to conceive of such a thing. Nevertheless, Hume argues, men are so nearly equal in bodily force ('and even in their mental powers till cultivated by education'), that 'nothing but their own consent could, at first, associate them together, and subject them to any authority'. The potential advantages of such authority are reasonably evident – namely, peace and order – and provided a sufficient motive as well as sufficiently obvious conditions (which need not have been made explicit) for submission. In this sense, Hume accepts the contention that government was first founded on an original contract (HTP, 195–6).

Yet Hume entirely rejected the contractarian account of political obligation and legitimate political authority. More precisely, consent or contract is for Hume a sufficient ground for such obligation and authority, but by no means a necessary one. And this is fortunate, since no *existing* government was founded on voluntary compact; the original contract has been 'obliterated by a thousand changes of government and princes', with the result that 'almost all the governments which exist at present, or of which there remains any record . . . have been founded . . . either on usurpation or conquest'. Once government became established, in other words, the approximately equal natural strength of men ceased to be relevant; as organisations of superior force governments could and did impose their will regardless of 'consent'. This applies not only to governments established by conquest, but to stable, 'legitimate' government also. But what of the Lockean notion that 'by living under the dominion of a prince, which one might leave, every individual has given a *tacit* consent to his authority, and promised him obedience'? Hume deals with this suggestion in devastating fashion. There can be no consent and no promise where there is no *choice*; but no one (philosophers apart) who is born under an established government supposes he has any choice in this matter. Objectively speaking, only a minority at best could have any choice.

'Can we seriously say that a poor peasant or artisan has a free choice to leave his country, when he knows no foreign language or manners, and lives from day to day, by the small wages which he acquires? We may as well assert that a man, by remaining in a vessel, freely consents to the dominion of the master, though he was carried on board while asleep, and must leap into the ocean, and perish, the moment he leaves her.' (HTP, 196–9, 203)

In sum, if legitimate political authority depended on contract or prior consent of the governed, it would be more or less non-existent in the present age.

To Hume that is a *reductio ad absurdum* of the contract theory. Most existing governments *are* legitimate, men have an obligation to obey them, and the reason is simple: *because society could not otherwise subsist* (HTP, 209) (and without society, individuals could not subsist). In other words, Hume aims to destroy a fundamental presupposition of all contract theory from Engelbert of Volkersdorf onwards, by showing that the way in which government originated among men (by consent or even contract) is a quite separate question from why we should (or should not) obey it. This is true, even although the *reasons* why men first accepted government are exactly the same as the reasons why they should obey it now – for the sake of peaceful and orderly society. To Hume it is these reasons that really determine obligation, not contract, even in cases where a contract of sorts might have occurred. But, as a matter of fact, it is dubious whether Hume should, from his point of view, have allowed the reality even of the 'original contract'. What he agrees to call by that name is a voluntary acquiescence in the first assertions of political authority; but such mere acquiescence does not seem capable of expressing a *specific future commitment* to obey, and thus differs from a contract, as understood by all contract theorists.

If we now consider the critiques of Filmer and of Hume together, their joint burden is either to deny the occurrence of any social contract, whether the original contract or later reaffirmations thereof, or else at least to deny the occurrence of any contract relevant, in historical times, to political obligation. In assessing the effectiveness of these criticisms, we must consider two questions: (1) Are the critics right when they deny that governments have really been founded on contracts? (2) If they are, does this fact completely discredit social contract theory? As for the first of these two questions, it is necessary to distinguish between different forms of contract theory. Perhaps the most plausible, as a strictly historical account, is that of Althusius, which envisages the union of individuals into families and other private associations, of private associations into lesser public associations and of the lesser public associations into commonwealths. Althusius also incorporated the ancient concept of a contract between the people and its (future) ruler, both at the institution of the state and at the election of a new prince; and this element is not only plausible, but is even a reasonable interpretation of the constitution of some medieval European kingdoms. Nevertheless, as history, the Althusian theory suffers from several defects. First, the plausibility of the contract between people and ruler depends on one's willingness to allow that the people can act through representatives, and its accuracy as history requires that certain magnates, not delegated by the people, may be considered as occupying this representative role. Here, it is hard not to side with Filmer in rejecting such a notion. Second, it would not be sufficient if the constitutions of some particular medieval states did indeed incorporate a contract between ruler and people – for contract theory claims to be a *general* theory of legitimate government. And third, a degree of plausibility is not the same thing as actual historicity, and while the Althusian sequence of events may not be too implausible, this is not to say that it actually occurred (the sequence in its Aristotelian version, as a *natural* progression, may well seem the more plausible of the two).

As an account of the history of states, then, even the Althusian version of the contract theory, and the ancient notion of a contract between people and ruler which it incorporates, are highly imperfect. And the problems on this score are much greater for the 'classical' version of contract theory, which portrays the state as a creation of numerous individuals (or heads of families) contracting together, and supposes that subsequent generations of citizens adhere, one by one, to the original contract. Here the scepticism of Filmer and Hume as to the reality of such contracts seems highly persuasive. In sum, our answer to question (1) must be, Yes, the critics are right.

But let us now turn to the more important question (2). Actually, several different questions arise under this heading. In the first place, let us briefly reconsider Hume's critique. If we accept the reality of the original contract, and the original contract only, is Hume right to proclaim the irrelevance of this contract to present political obligation? In my view he is, but nevertheless some considerations on the other side of the question should be noted. Hume is clearly right that no existing state is directly founded on an original contract; nevertheless, one should consider separately the problems arising from 'usurpation and conquest' on the one hand, and from the peaceful continuation of states through successive generations on the other. It is, after all, open to the contract theorist to deny the legitimacy of states founded immediately or ultimately on violence, precisely on the ground that such states are not based on consent (Locke did just this) – and while to Hume this leads to absurd (indeed dangerous) results, everyone is not compelled to agree with him. This remains an open question. It would be more difficult to deny the legitimacy of states which, at first founded on an original contract, continue peacefully through successive generations. Locke, as we know, did not wish to do so. Here the question is: does the logic of contract theory nevertheless require such a denial? Hume, I believe, has shown that it does, so far as the standard form of the theory is concerned (this is an important qualification, as we shall see shortly). Yet it must be admitted that, none the less, commonsense assumptions about the legitimacy of political regimes are on the side of contract theory here. It *is* a widespread assumption that if a state was first founded in a legitimate way, then it continues to be legitimate so long as it continues in the same form. For example, it is widely held that the federal constitution of the United States of America is legitimate *today*, because it was agreed by legitimate procedures involving the representatives of the people involved in 1787 (and in later years, when other states acceded). No one would dream of questioning the legitimacy of the American government's authority on the grounds that later generations of citizens have been given no opportunity to consent to it; the (indirect) consent of the first generation is acknowledged to be sufficient, as well as (many would hold) necessary for this legitimacy. It takes the penetration of a Hume to show that this kind of thinking is sloppy and untenable.

The reality of the original contract, if this is granted, is thus not enough to validate contract theory; and in any case we have seen that it too may well be denied. In this case the entire notion that government is founded on contract is fictitious; a fact which is indeed fatal to contract theory in its standard form, that is, from Manegold to Locke. It is worth repeating why this is so. The theory of social contract, in its standard form, holds that the political obligation of peoples and individuals, and the limits of that obligation, derive from undertakings that they (and perhaps also their rulers) have voluntarily given. If they have not, in fact, given any such undertakings, no conclusions about their obligations can be derived in this way. However, one at least of the contract theorists whom we have discussed may be unaffected (or at least undamaged) by this criticism – namely Rousseau. For Rousseau, no less than Hume, though for quite different reasons, refused to found political obligation on what he took to be the terms and conditions of the actual original contract – that contract, we saw, he held to be the outcome of selfishness, cunning and folly (in brief, of corruption). The contract from which he derived the terms of political obligation was not the actual, but an ideal contract. It is true that he does not say so explicitly, but this (as we argued above) seems the most natural interpretation of his meaning. If this is correct, and if Rousseau also holds, as he seems to (R, 173,249), that actual prior consent is necessary to obligation, the implication is that no one has, or will have, any political obligation until the ideal contract is made (if ever). Precisely this may be the implication that Rousseau intended. But, there is also, let us note, an alternative view that one might derive from Rousseau's ideal contract; namely, that men's obligation depends, not on what they *have* promised, but rather on what, ideally, they *ought* to have promised, which presumably is not much different from what they ought to be prepared to promise, now. In other words, men would on this interpretation be obliged to obey political institutions conforming to the ideal contract, regardless of any actual contract. This is an interpretation that puts social contract theory in an altogether new light. It has the advantage of undercutting certain obvious criticisms of the theory, such as Hume's, but, as we shall see later, it also creates new problems.

Ideal and hypothetical contract: Kant

It is not likely that Rousseau's formulation of contract theory was influenced by the arguments of Hume. The last of the eighteenth century contract theorists to be considered, however, was certainly influenced by both Hume and Rousseau. This is the German philosopher Immanuel Kant. In Kant's version, the social contract is for the first time clearly and explicitly stated to be, not an actual event, but a regulatory ideal, or, in Kant's words, an 'idea of reason'. By this he means, roughly, that, although political institutions have certainly not derived from such a contract in fact, the idea of a social contract can and should be used to test their rightness; they should be such that they *could* have been agreed to by all subject to them, 'could have been produced by the united will of a whole nation' (K, 79). This non-actual version of the social contract appears to be somewhat different from Rousseau's – it appears, one might say, to be a *hypothetical* rather than an *ideal* contract (what men could have agreed to, rather than what they ought to have agreed to). But we shall see shortly that this difference may be more apparent than real.

In one way, Kant's conception of the social contract as nothing but an idea of reason considerably weakens its impact; but on the other hand, it greatly broadens its scope. Kant's idea of reason, to repeat, is a criterion of rightness in matters political, but it is not a criterion of political obligation. Kant recoils from Rousseau's bold dictum that only derivation from, or conformity to, the (ideal) social contract makes man's political 'chains' legitimate, and still more from his implicit conclusion that we have no obligation to obey powers not legitimate in this sense.[8] Rather, for Kant the idea of the possible social contract is to be taken as a guide by legislators and rulers; it is certainly not to be used by subjects as an excuse for resistance or disobedience. But if Kant's application of the contractarian idea is in this way relatively timid, in another way it is markedly ambitious. The idea of testing political institutions by their conformity to a possible contract of all those subject to them can be very widely applied; and Kant applied it in a considerable variety of ways.

In the first place, Kant uses it to validate the existence of the state as such. The 'idea' of the original contract, he says, alone allows us to conceive of the state as legitimate (K, 140); in other words, the state is a legitimate institution because we can conceive that individuals *could* agree to accept its authority (it being irrelevant whether they *have* done so). Secondly, the idea of the social contract provides a criterion for the *ideal constitution* of the state. On what constitution would or could all who are to be subject to it unanimously agree? Unfortunately, Kant, who is not the most lucid of writers, does not seem to give a completely clear or consistent answer to this. His answer appears to be that legislation should be by the decision of a majority of citizens, or rather (at least in a large state) a majority of representatives of the citizens – what Kant calls a republican constitution. But he also asserts that the necessary qualification for citizenship is ability to support oneself without depending on others, and uses this criterion to exclude from citizenship 'those who are merely labourers' (including 'the domestic servant, the shop assistant, . . . even the barber') as well as women (K, 77–9,163,139–40). The notion that women and 'mere labourers' would agree to this (if that is indeed Kant's contention) does not seem very plausible. But be that as it may, Kant's use of the social contract both to justify the state and to prescribe its constitution is quite in line with the arguments of his predecessors Hobbes, Locke, and Rousseau.

Kant, however, goes further than these writers by also using the 'idea' of the social contract as a test of the justice of laws. Laws are to be framed in such a way that they could be consented to by every subject – or rather, citizen (a more restricted category, as we saw above). This entails, Kant claims, that all subjects (or citizens?) should be equal before the law; there should be no hereditary legal privileges for favoured groups ('every member of the commonwealth must be entitled to reach any degree of rank which a subject can earn through his talent, his industry and his good fortune'); there should not be unequal taxation of subjects of the same class; and so on (K, 79,74–5). Kant also lays down a principle of equal freedom ('each may seek his happiness in whatever way he sees fit, so long as he does not infringe upon the freedom of others to pursue a similar end which can be reconciled with the freedom of everyone else within a workable general law'), but whether he claims to derive this principle from the idea of the social contract is unclear (K, 74). But in one field he does derive a bold and original conclusion from that premise, namely in international relations. The existing relation of states is lawless, devoid of justice, essentially a relation of war. In accordance with the idea of the social contract, 'it is necessary to establish a federation of peoples', or rather a confederation – *not* a sovereign authority 'as in a civil constitution', but an alliance, such that 'states will protect one another against external aggression while refraining from interference in one another's internal disagreements' (K, 165). Ideas similar to these underlie the League of Nations and United Nations in our own time.

We have noted above some equivocations on points of detail in Kant's application of his version of contract theory; but we must now turn our attention to a more fundamental ambiguity. Kant's proposal, we saw above, was to test the rightness of political institutions by whether or not they could have been agreed to in a social contract. But, we may ask, how useful a test is this? Is the criterion 'what could have been agreed' a useful one? Offhand, one might think that almost anything *could* have been agreed. It is true that Kant claims that this criterion prescribes certain specific institutions, such as the 'republican constitution', and still more that it excludes others, such as hereditary legal privileges; but exactly how Kant derives these conclusions from his contractarian premises is not at once obvious. The fact of the matter is that Kant is not perspicuous here, but let us try to reconstruct his meaning. Glossing his criterion 'what could have been agreed by the whole people', Kant explains that he means this literally – he doesn't mean what they *would* agree to in their present 'position or attitude of mind' (K, 79). But what, then, *is* the relevant 'position' and 'attitude of mind' in terms of which hypothetical agreement is to be assessed? Why, for example, does the contractarian test proscribe hereditary legal privileges? At first glance, the answer might appear to be, because such privileges could never be accepted by the disprivileged, from the standpoint of their self-interest. To adopt the standpoint of the self-interest of (actual or hypothetical) contractors would be thoroughly in accord with the social contract tradition in general; but in fact this cannot be Kant's intention. In one place, he writes that it is the duty of rulers to govern in a way consonant with laws 'which a people of *mature rational powers* would prescribe for itself' (emphasis added) (K, 187). Now, these words in themselves do not preclude adopting the standpoint of self-interest, for there is no necessary contradiction between self-interest and rationality (and in earlier contract theorists, notably Hobbes, they were closely united). But it is beyond question that that is *not* Kant's understanding of rationality. In brief, rationality is for him co-extensive with morality, and hence cannot be reconciled with purely self-interested motivation. Hence we arrive at Kant's true view of the matter. In general, he says, contracts uniting large groups of men are 'for some common end which they all share'; but the *pactum unionis civilis* (contract of civil union) is exceptional, referring to an end 'which they all *ought to share'*. It is thus a *duty* to accept the state (K, 73,137). Here, clearly, Kant refers to what *fully moral* individuals would accept. In a similar way he is able to use the idea of the social contract to specify not just an acceptable constitution for the state, but an ideal constitution (and one which excludes some persons from citizenship). In the end, then, Kant's version of the social contract appears to be, like Rousseau's, not just a hypothetical, but an ideal contract.

The distinction between a hypothetical and an ideal social contract is an important one, and in one respect the former seems to be much the more valid concept of the two (we are now assuming that the idea of an actual social contract is discredited). To invoke an ideal contract is to appeal to what individuals, ideally, ought to agree to, or what they would agree to if they were ideally moral beings. As a way of arguing for or against particular political institutions, this seems needlessly circuitous. In brief, morally good beings would agree to morally good institutions, and whatever arguments might be deployed to show that institutions are such that morally good beings would (or would not) agree to them, could be deployed directly in defence of (or against) the institutions themselves, without reference to agreement, contract, or consent. The case of hypothetical contract is different, and is indeed available as a possible way of reformulating the whole social contract tradition up to Locke (and perhaps Rousseau also). Thus interpreted, social contract theorists are understood to assert that, in certain circumstances considered to be relevant to determining political obligation, individuals or peoples *would agree* to government according to certain terms (or perhaps better, would be willing to agree). The typical circumstance of this hypothetical agreement, in contract theory, is, of course, the state of nature, that is, a condition where men lack centralised government. On the present interpretation, the state of nature too could be considered to be a purely imaginable or hypothetical state of affairs, or as a possible one, or even as perhaps once actual.

The notion of deriving political obligation from what men would agree to in a state of nature, while avoiding some of the difficulties of the actual and the ideal social contracts, still faces some old problems as well as some new ones. One problem is that such an argument is inevitably speculative (though no more so than arguments about supposedly actual contracts of which no record remains). Both this hypothetical contract, and the supposedly actual but unrecorded contract, in effect depend on postulates about *human nature* – a universal human nature which motivates a universal contract and so generates universal principles of political obligation. Arguments on this score are liable to be somewhat treacherous. Is it even clear that human nature is such as to generate the necessary agreement at all? In fact, social contract theorists have relied not so much on actual human nature as on an idealised model of it. By this I do not mean a conception of human nature as ideally moral; on the contrary, the basic assumption (explicit or implicit) has been that the (hypothetical) contractors are motivated by self-interest. They expect to be better off under government, appropriately constituted. But can sheer self-interest produce agreement? The assumption of contract theorists (explicit or implicit) is that it will do so, if the contractors are *rational* in their pursuit of self-interest. Thus conceived, the terms of political obligation are determined by the political institutions that rational, self-interested agents would agree to submit to, in a state of nature. In this way, a *moral* obligation of obedience is derived from a hypothetical agreement motivated by self-interest. On this interpretation, Hobbes's theory, for example, can be summarised as claiming that we have a *moral* obligation of (nearly) absolute obedience to the sovereign, because it is in our interest that such a (nearly) absolute sovereign exists. The hypothetical interpretation of the social contract leads us from what was agreed by all, to what is in the interest of all, as the ground of obligation. However, this latter notion still requires some clarification, since there is nothing that is likely to be in the interest of all, *compared with all possible alternatives*. The alternative postulated by the social contract theory of political obligation is the non-political condition, the state of nature. And here we encounter a new problem, for it is not self-evident why just *this* is the appropriate benchmark for comparison; a problem which would not arise if, having actually been in a state of nature, we had actually made a contract to submit to government.

What is essentially the same problem can be put in a different way. It is perhaps not hard to show that a given form of state is more advantageous for everyone than no state at all (though even this the anarchists, by definition, would deny). But there may be many such forms of state. How, then, can this mode of reasoning show which is the legitimate or best form of state, as contract theory down the centuries has sought to do? Just this difficulty accounts for the huge variety of state forms and constitutions that have been defended by different contract theorists – a variety which has been exemplified in the pages of this book, and is symptomatic of the problematic character of the contractarian idea.

6 A Defence of Contract Theory against Some of its Critics

Fifty years ago a distinguished historian of the social contract, J. W. Gough, wrote that Kant's political philosophy 'brings us within sight of the end of the history of the contract theory' (Gough, 1957, p.181). Recent developments have shown this judgement to be premature, as we shall shortly illustrate at some length. Nevertheless, Gough had apparently good grounds for his remark. In the first place, it is true that after the time of Kant's writing (the end of the eighteenth century), contract theory went into eclipse, along with the theory of natural law with which it was so closely allied. This was, in part, a delayed result of the influence of Hume on the utilitarian philosophers whose style of thinking became predominant in Britain; in part, also, a consequence of the increasing tendency to consider society and politics historically, a vantage point from which the social contract idea seems highly dubious. One of the most important of the historicist critics of contract theory is the German philosopher, Hegel, about whom we shall have more to say below.

But Gough meant something more than this by his comment on Kant. Kant used the idea of the social contract, but recognised it to be a historical fiction. Thus, in effect, he admitted it to be superfluous, 'since political obligation could quite well be founded directly, without any interpolation of a contract, on the moral obligations' which he derived from his general moral theory. Yet the modern revival of contract theory, associated above all with the name of John Rawls, explicitly claims to adopt a Kantian (non-historical) conception of the contract; so it is worth considering whether Gough's verdict is justified. I believe that Gough is right, so far as concerns Kant's particular version of 'ideal' contract theory (as I termed it in the previous chapter). But the general charge of what we can call 'superfluousness' against all theories which invoke a non-historical social contract requires further consideration.

This charge has been made very frequently. Consider, for example, the theory of John Locke. Hannah Pitkin, in a well-known paper which discusses Locke's difficulties in giving a plausible account of 'tacit' consent, concludes that what matters to Locke is not really whether one has consented or contracted to obey a government, but whether the government *deserves* one's consent. And this, in turn, is determined by the law of nature, which government has a duty to respect and enforce. Governments should be obeyed if, and only if, they protect their subjects' lives, liberty and property, which are their natural rights – a fact known to us by reason, Locke claims, and not dependent on any contract. So the contract and consent which bulk so large in his theory are, it appears, superfluous (Pitkin, 1965, pp.995–9).

I believe this analysis fails to grasp the specific significance of the idea of the contract in Locke's theory and (I would like to suggest) in all contract theories. It does *not* follow from the fact that the law of nature imposes such-and-such obligations, or creates certain rights, that anyone has an obligation to obey an individual or organisation that seeks to enforce that natural law. There might be innumerable such individuals or organisations, whose competing efforts would produce precisely the negative features of the Lockean state of nature. What Locke's contractarian argument seeks to show is that every individual has an interest in agreeing to the establishment of a single, exclusive, centralised agency of law-enforcement: the state. It is from this argument, which appeals to the self-interest of all individuals, not (or not only) to the law of nature, that Locke would derive political obligation and its limits. In this respect he is typical of contract theorists in general. (Notice that anarchists will reject this or any other contractarian argument, even although they may perfectly well agree with Locke about the law of nature). Needless to say, this understanding of contract theory does not render it unproblematic – as indicated in the last chapter, there remain the questions of why superiority over the state of nature should be considered the decisive test of political institutions, and of what exactly that test legitimates in any case. But I think we can reject the charge that contract theory, in its hypothetical form, is vacuous.

Hegel and his successors

If the specific meaning of contract theory is, as suggested, the derivation of political obligation from the self-interest of individuals, then just this very feature has been the object of a highly influential attack, from the nineteenth-century German philosopher, Hegel. According to Hegel, a contract theory of the state rests on an utter misapprehension of the state's true nature. The nature of contract, to Hegel, is clear enough. Individuals are free to make contracts in regard to whatever is their own property; contracts result from a coincidence of individual wills, what Hegel calls a 'common will' of the parties (HR, 57–9). Contract is appropriate to, and characteristic of, the sphere of human activity which Hegel calls 'civil society', a term which, in significant contrast to many contractarian thinkers, he distinguishes from 'the state', and which for him includes, notably, economic transactions. In civil society 'the particular person is essentially so related to other particular persons that each . . . finds satisfaction by means of the others'; it is at once a system of 'interdependence', and of the 'attainment of selfish ends'. Thus contracts in this sphere typically, and legitimately, result not just from a common will of individuals, but from a coincidence of their self-interest (HR, 122–3,126).

The mistake of contract theory, according to Hegel, is to conceive of the state as if it were an aspect of civil society. 'The state', he asserts, 'is not a contract at all, nor is its fundamental essence the unconditional protection and guarantee of the life and property of members of the public as individuals'. To suppose that it is, Hegel suggests, is grossly to underrate the value of the state as such, to deny its true 'majesty and absolute authority', even (Hegel says) its divinity. It is only membership in the state which gives the individual his true individuality. The state is far too important to be considered the property of its individual members, or a mere means to advance their ends. Membership of the state is not, for the individual, something 'optional' (as the contractarian idiom suggests), but is his 'supreme duty'. Hence the state has 'supreme right *against* the individual' (emphasis added); as a 'higher entity', it is entitled to demand of the individual the sacrifice of his 'very life and property' (HR, 71,156–57).

This is not the whole of Hegel's objection to contract theory, but it is convenient to consider now the argument outlined above. At first glance, it does not seem convincing. In spite of the exalted, not to say bombastic, language applied to the state by Hegel, it remains unclear just what alternative to the interests of individuals he proposes to offer as the justification of its authority or the criterion of its constitution. At one point, indeed, he seems (despite himself) almost to allow an individualistic justification – that membership in the state is a necessary condition of the genuine individuality of individuals. This, to be sure, is a disputable and somewhat obscure claim; but if we take it to mean that only as a member of a state can a person realise his full human potential, then that is certainly the invocation of an individualistic criterion. Yet if the state is entitled to demand the sacrifice of the individual's very life, his individuality cannot after all be the justification of the state. Rather, it looks as if Hegel's argument is that, because the individual derives his individuality from the state, therefore he owes it his life *in return* – as if the state were a kind of superior being to which this supreme duty of gratitude is owed, just as Christians might hold the individual owes a similar duty to the God who created him. Not for nothing does Hegel call the state 'divine'.

We might well dismiss this 'divine state' argument as nothing better than obfuscating mysticism, but for one thing. Perhaps Hegel is right to say that (on occasions at least) the state is entitled to demand that individuals must sacrifice their lives for it. Indeed, very many states apparently act on this assumption, by conscripting citizens into their armed forces to fight – and risk death – in battle. Hegel, as it happens, considered war to be an essential and desirable element in human progress (HR, 209–11), but it is not necessary to share this view in order to accept that there are *some* occasions when a state would be right to fight a war (for example, in self-defence) and thus to require some of its citizens to sacrifice their lives therein. Our question now is: can the social contract theory of political authority be reconciled with this? If the state is to be justified as a means to the ends of its individual citizens – if its authority depends on what it would be in the interest of all subject to that authority to agree to – can its authority include this sacrifice of the lives of individuals? A similar problem is raised by the issue of capital punishment. The eighteenth century Italian penal reformer, Beccaria, argued that, just because in a social contract men could never agree to establish a state that might execute them, capital punishment is illegitimate (Gough, 1957, p.175). For Hegel, Beccaria's deduction from contract theory is correct, but shows the absurdity of the theory (HR, 70–1).

At this point it is worth considering what some major contract theorists have had to say about these issues. Both Hobbes and Locke, for example, agreed with Hegel that the state may legitimately inflict capital punishment; but not because the state is a being more exalted than mere individuals. Locke's argument is that the right to punish breaches of the law is a right *of all men in a state of nature*; the state derives this right (including the right to use the death penalty) from the individuals, who by yielding it up to a central authority, leave the state of nature and enter civil society (L, 6,43–4). In other words, liability to capital punishment is for Locke a concomitant of the law of nature (or of its breach); it is not affected by the social contract, except that this contract *limits* the agencies entitled to inflict it. In this theory, the right of capital punishment, while not *derived* from the contract, is not incompatible with it either. But some critics have found Locke's argument here unsatisfactory. In brief, they deny that anything other than the state could ever have any general right of punishment at all. The ground of this right, they claim, is that punishment is necessary to maintain order and protect rights; but a right of punishment inhering in all men, in the absence of a centralised state, cannot achieve these objects – as Locke himself admits, since this is avowedly the reason for yielding up the general right of punishment. As one critic has put it: what can be the justification for a right so ineffective that it has to be given up? (Altham, 1979, pp.139–40; cf. Anscombe, 1981, pp.146f.). It looks, then, as if Locke's attempt to derive the state's right to punish from a similar original right of individuals is a failure.

As for Hobbes, he has less to say about the state's right of punishment than about the subject's duty to fight on its behalf in war. This duty is not absolute, according to Hobbes; just as a man cannot give up his right to defend his body against attack, so he cannot unconditionally undertake to expose it to attack in battle, whenever the sovereign so commands (though for Hobbes, of course, there is no injustice in such a command by a sovereign). However, there is one crucial case where a subject *is* obliged 'not only to go to the battle, but also not to run from it, without his captain's leave'; namely, 'when the defence of the Commonwealth, requireth at once the help of all that are able to bear arms ... ; because otherwise the institution of the Commonwealth [would be] in vain' (HL, 268–70). In other words, since the survival of the state is in the individual's interest, so too is an obligation to fight for it in a *defensive* war. As Hobbes might have said, such an obligation, while of course risky, 'is less hurtful than the want of it' (cf. p.55 above). And he could say exactly the same about punishment, including perhaps capital punishment. This seems to give a fully adequate answer to Hegel's objection to contract theory, as well as providing a far better criterion than Hegel's as to *when* the citizen is obliged to respond to the state's call to make the supreme sacrifice.

We can now safely reject Hegel's accusation that contract theory unduly exalts the dignity of the individual and his interests by comparison with those of the state. But before returning to Hegel's anti-contractarianism, let us look at another argument which, while less statist than Hegel's, is equally anti-individualist. This is due to Otto Gierke, whom we have already had occasion to honour as one of the greatest historians of contract theory. Despite his respect for the theory and for its major exponents, Gierke felt nevertheless that it fundamentally misconceived the true relation between the individual and the state. The theory of a contract of rulership, he felt, was never able to arrive at a real notion of the state at all, the state as a unity, that is, but always conceived it dualistically, as a combination of 'ruler' and 'people'; and even the later, 'classical' phase of contract theory also could not adequately conceptualise the state's unity, but saw it only as a 'collectivity' of individuals (or of lesser social units themselves collectivities of individuals or families), or else as their 'representative' (as in the case of Hobbes's sovereign). In either case, Gierke complains, the state is given a basically individualistic interpretation, ultimately resolving itself into an aggregate of mere legal connections between individuals. And this is wrong because, for Gierke, the state is an independent entity on its own account. It is, he suggests, an 'organic unity', even a 'person' with its own will and personality (GNL, 42f.,115,50–53).

Gierke's theory does not exalt the state as Hegel's did, for he applied it, not just to the state, but to social groups in general. Nevertheless, it seems that he does want to exalt the state *vis-à-vis* individuals more, at least, than he thinks is the case in social contract theory. Yet it is not easy to get to grips with Gierke's critique. While it presumably has normative implications, it is perhaps primarily to be understood as a sociological thesis, or rather one in the philosophy of social science – as an example, therefore, of the position known as logical or methodological holism, to be contrasted with the methodological individualism espoused more recently by writers such as Hayek and Popper. (Gierke, indeed, characterises the philosophical stance embodied in social contract theory as 'logical individualism') (GNL, 115). The general drift of sociological holism is to deny that social groups are to be identified with any combination of individuals; and if they are, in fact, themselves 'persons', presumably they may, for example, have rights that cannot be identified with, or justified in terms of, the rights or interests of any individual or individuals. There is no space here for an adequate discussion of these issues (I have in fact considered them elsewhere).[1] Suffice it, for present purposes, to say that if the reader is persuaded by this holistic interpretation of social groups, he will be sympathetic to Gierke's objections to contract theory; and if not, not. Personally I am unpersuaded. But Gierke does have this merit: he makes clear that the rejection of methodological individualism means denying not only that social groups are aggregates of individuals, but also that they are to be understood in terms of *relations between* individuals. He thus, to my mind, shows up the implausibility of the still widely-held holistic doctrine.

Let us now return to Hegel. There is no reason to be impressed by his extreme statism, which we have already discussed, but Hegel has another reason for objecting to social contract theory, and one which cannot be dismissed so quickly. This is his attack on the concept of the state of nature, which is such an integral part of contract theory in its classic form; it is men in a state of nature who make the contract. Hegel does not believe the state of nature ever existed, but this is not the crucial point, not, that is, if we are considering contract theory in its hypothetical version. Even in this version, the theory involves a deduction from what it would be in the interest of individuals in the state of nature to agree to. It thus depends crucially on postulates of *universal* human nature, and in two ways: it is this universal human nature that will determine the characteristics of the state of nature (a state of war, or whatever), and also will motivate men to contract out of it. But this whole conception, according to Hegel, is nothing but a 'nebulous' theoretical abstraction without any reality, and a thoroughly misleading one. Man is a social and historical being, his individuality determined by his particular culture. Not only does he always exist within a particular society and culture (Volk) that differs from others, and at a particular period of historical development, but any attempt to distil out of this human diversity a constant and unchanging 'essence' of man is bound to be totally arbitrary (HN, 63–5; HH, 54–6). Man shorn of his culturally determined attributes ceases to be man.

It is important to understand just what the problem is that this argument from the social nature of man creates for social contract theory, for many of its critics seem to me to have misunderstood it. A modern example, I believe, is Hannah Pitkin, whose well-known writings were referred to above. Pitkin objects to theories that base political obligation on individuals' consent (and this of course includes contract theories) on grounds similar to those just outlined. We are all moulded by society, and the interests, desires, and so on, which the consent (and contract) theorist postulates as motives for the consent that he so exalts are not our own creation but come from social influences: 'our selves are manifestly social' (Pitkin, 1966, p.46). Hence, Pitkin concludes, we have obligations (to 'society'?) irrespective of our consent.

It is true that individuals have obligations that are independent of their consent; but Pitkin's argument from the social nature of man does nothing to establish this (and in particular fails to establish that *political* obligation is independent of consent). If we reject the Gierkean notion that society is a personality separable from its individual members, then all our obligations are owed to individuals, and obligations 'to society' are simply obligations to its members. What then is the bearing of man's social nature on these obligations? At this point Pitkin seems to conflate, in a way that is rather common, two different kinds of relationship. All of us owe a great deal to certain of our fellows – notably our parents, and other benefactors – and, arguably, we therefore have corresponding consent-independent obligations to them. In addition to this, we – and our parents and benefactors too – are part of a complex matrix of relations between individuals (which, loosely speaking, constitutes 'society') by which everybody is greatly influenced and which, to a large extent, makes the individual what he is. This is the social nature of man. But from this general *causal* nexus nothing follows about obligations; it can seem to do so only by conflating it with the benefits which each person receives from other specific persons, which do (arguably) generate obligations. The conflation is the easier, in that those to whom we normally owe most – our parents – are also perhaps the primary channel through which social influences shape us. (None of this, incidentally, is meant to show that we have no obligations to those from whom we have received no benefits; but these obligations have nothing to do with the fact that we are shaped by social influences). So far as political obligation is concerned, Pitkin would have been on much stronger ground if she had argued that it derives from receipt of benefit rather than from our social nature.

The bearing of obligation arising from receipt of benefit on contract theory is a theme that will be taken up later. Meanwhile, let us remind ourselves of the real reason why man's social nature raises problems for contract theory. That theory standardly rests on an assumption of a universal human nature, from which a universal contract can be derived. Yet if man is essentially social, and human societies are historically and culturally *diverse*, then human nature will appear to be radically diverse also. The model of man used in social contract theory thus risks, as was said above, being not only unreal but arbitrary – what is taken to be human nature may be only one of innumerable possible human natures, and the temptation is great to construct the model just in such a way as to generate the desired conclusions. We have already referred to the great variety of contradictory political conclusions derived from contractarian premises – all of which, however, claim universal validity.

Social contract theory as ideology

In order to proceed to the next stage of our analysis, we must remind ourselves that contract theories vary not only in their conclusions, but also in their premises. In medieval times the predominant premise of the theory was the contract between people and ruler; ever since the seventeenth century, however, the characteristic starting-point (for philosophers if not for politicians) has been the contracting individual. Generally speaking, the proposal to understand contract theory hypothetically refers to this individualistic contract theory, as do the criticisms of contract theory that we have considered in this chapter. What follows refers specifically to the individualistic kind of contract theory, on which two lines of attack seem to emerge from our discussion so far. In a sense they seem almost contrary to one another; yet we shall see that they merge into a single critique: the claim that social contract theory is *ideological*.

Individualistic social contract theories share a common starting point – the 'abstract' individual – but arrive at various conclusions because (it may be charged) the 'abstract' individual is a vacuous concept which the theorist may fill in as he pleases. One line of attack is on what all such theories have in common – the postulate of the 'abstract' individual; another is on the openness of this postulate to arbitrary manipulation (which renders the theories diverse). The two lines of attack come together, however, in the notion that one, historically specific, type of society, more than others, approximates (or appears to approximate) to a collection of individuals, and that contract theorists characteristically understand (or misunderstand) the nature of the human individual *per se* in terms of the characteristics of members of this type of society. Individualistic contract theory, in brief, is on this account a product, a reflection and a justification of 'individualistic' society; which latter may also be called liberal society, market society, or capitalism. So viewed contract theory appears as an *ideology* of this form of society.

The concept of ideology is a part of the Marxist theory of society, according to which ideas are generally a reflection of social (ultimately economic) reality, and dominant ideas reflect the position, interests and world-view of the dominant social class. These interests are, however, characteristically presented as universal interests. Thus ideologies are systematically one-sided and misleading. It is obvious that the theory of ideology provides a ready method of attacking contract theory. Of the writers to be considered in this section of our discussion, some are indeed Marxists, while those who are not have undoubtedly been influenced by the Marxist theory.

Let us begin by considering the argument developed by C. B. Macpherson in his famous book, *The Political Theory of Possessive Individualism*. Macpherson here considers two great seventeenth century contract theorists, Hobbes and Locke, but we shall confine ourselves to his analysis of Hobbes, which seems more germane to social contract theory in general. In brief, Macpherson discerns two significant parallels between the premises of Hobbes's theory, and the social reality of the English society of the time, which Macpherson describes as a 'possessive market society' (that is, a capitalist society). According to Hobbes, the natural relation of men is a relation of fundamental equality, and a relation of intrinsic competition for power. Macpherson stresses that for Hobbes the fundamental equality of man is not an equality of natural right – that is derivative from a fundamental *factual* equality of condition, in fact an equal vulnerability to the invasions of others. This natural equality in insecurity, and natural competitiveness for power over others, are the basic premises from which Hobbes deduces his contract theory. According to Macpherson's interpretation, both premises reflect features, not of the human condition as such, but of possessive market society, of capitalism. It is subservience to the capitalist market and its vagaries which creates for everyone a basic equality of insecurity; it is in the capitalist market that men compete to exercise power by controlling other men. In no other form of economic system is this so; in a traditional hierarchical society, for example, while certainly some men exercise power over others, the distinctions between superiors and inferiors are fixed – there is no universal competitive struggle, no equality in insecurity (Macpherson, 1962, pp.68–70,87–8). Though Macpherson does not exactly say so, it appears as if he sees the natural freedom of men postulated by Hobbes as grounded also in this universal competitiveness of the capitalist market economy – a freedom to compete for power, to invade others (ibid., pp.53–60, 100). In any case an analysis similar to Macpherson's analysis of Hobbes can quite easily be extended to social contract theory more generally. Thus a later commentator, Carole Pateman, has suggested that the 'free and equal' individuals who populate the contractarians' state of nature reflect the (formally?) free and equal individuals required for the operation of the market, in which, indeed, contract is a central mode of relationship between agents. In these economic contracts, agents are assumed to be actuated by self-interest, just as they are in social contract theory (Pateman 1979, pp.50,169). Thus for both Macpherson and Pateman, the political arrangements defended by Hobbes and Locke on contractarian grounds are those which are needed to stabilise capitalist society and which appear legitimate to those who accept its operational principles.

From all of this arise a number of different though overlapping issues. I propose first to consider Macpherson's account of Hobbes. It is, in my opinion, more ingenious than convincing. What, one wonders, entitles Macpherson so firmly to set aside Hobbes's own avowed interpretation of the 'natural condition of mankind'? Macpherson, of course, is correct to point to Hobbes's stress on the *factual* equality of all men, and on their equal vulnerability to invasion by others. But according to Hobbes this equality of vulnerability is simply a consequence of men's *physical* constitution, and it is significant because of their propensity to attack one another *physically* in competition for power and glory. This is a much more fundamental competitiveness of the human condition than any to be found in the capitalist market. As for an empirical source for Hobbes's interpretations of human nature, why is it necessary to look further than the English Civil War, and the whole history of human warfare? Macpherson's assumption that its source must be found in some appropriate economic system seems a classic example of begging the question.[2] Rather, Hobbes seems heir to a long tradition of speculation about government, which saw it as the necessary remedy for the human propensity for self-destructive fighting, a tradition from which he differs only in his much greater precision and clarity of analysis, and which he passed on to his contractarian successors.

Macpherson's argument, then, seems to me unsuccessful. Nevertheless, this by no means disposes of the whole idea of social contract theory, or at any rate individualistic contract theory, as an ideology of capitalism. Other arguments to that effect can be, and have been, mounted. It is, besides, undeniable that contract theory did, in the early modern era, shift from a predominantly non-individualistic to a predominantly individualistic form, and that this individualistic form is the 'classical' form of the theory, the form in which it became, for at least two centuries, the predominant idiom of political philosophy. It is certainly legitimate to wonder, at the very least, whether this development may not have some connection with contemporary transformations of the economic and social structure in a capitalistic direction. In this regard, too, it is striking to find a prominent modern defender of capitalism, Sir Keith Joseph, extolling 'the idea of the state of nature, so beloved of eighteenth century political theorists'. This idea, he admits, is a myth, but 'it expresses an important truth', namely that 'men are so constituted that it is natural to them to pursue private rather than public ends'. Thus 'a society of autonomous individuals is the natural condition of mankind'; and, Sir Keith concludes, 'the duty of governments is to accommodate themselves to this immutable fact of human nature' (Joseph and Sumption, 1979, p.100). With this in mind, let us consider another argument to the effect that contract theory accords with a capitalist view of human nature.

The argument is that of the distinguished Soviet legal theorist Evgeny Pashukanis. According to Pashukanis law itself (probably he has in mind civil law rather than criminal law) is a reflection of a particular social form, namely the relationship between 'possessors of goods'. It presupposes an 'atomized economy', one which has the consequence that 'society itself seems to be an endless chain of juridic relationships between individuals. These individuals are conceived as the possessors of legal rights; law itself specifies the conditions of functioning of an individualistic society based on a capitalist economy (P, 138,140,166–7). So far, Pashukanis's analysis is a sociology of law. But he goes further. The doctrine of *natural* law (so closely allied to social contract theory) extends to the sphere of political philosophy the conceptions of individualistic private law. Hence Pashukanis's verdict that 'the natural law school was the most brilliant exponent of bourgeois ideology' and nurtured 'the great classics of bourgeois political science': works which purported to lay down standards ('the natural conditions of existence', as Pashukanis puts it) for society as such, but really formulated the standards ('conditions of existence') of bourgeois society (P, 127,188).

These are the terms in which Pashukanis interprets social contract theory: 'the natural law doctrine produces a state out of a contract of separate and isolated individuals'. Clearly, then, social contract theory is for Pashukanis a bourgeois ideology. And the individual contractors of individualist contract theory are not only separate and isolated, they are also held to be naturally free and equal – like participants in a market economy. Social contract theory extends to the sphere of political authority, as a basic premise, the freedom and equality that characterise the subject of rights in private law; a freedom and equality, ultimately, of the possessor of goods engaged in acts of exchange with other goods possessors. According to bourgeois conceptions, the legitimacy of transactions depends on a coincidence of wills of the individuals involved – in other words, on contract. Social contract theory reproduces this conception in the sphere of political authority (P, 188,149,164,155–6).

What exactly does Pashukanis mean by calling this theory a bourgeois ideology? Partly, as we have seen, that it proposes as a universal norm that which is normative only for capitalist society (and is to that extent delusive). But the concept of ideology is more complex than this. According to Pashukanis, the theory *both reflects and distorts* the reality of capitalist society (P, 183). We have already seen, at least in a general way, how it reflects it: the isolated, free and equal individuals who make the social contract reflect the isolated, free and equal possessors of goods whose contracts structure a capitalist economy. Or rather, an ideal rather than a real capitalist economy. For, in reality, the 'free and equal goods possessors meeting in the market are free only in the abstract relationship of acquisition and alienation' – free and equal, that is, only in their equal legal right freely to acquire and alienate property. In real life, far from being free and equal, they are bound to one another by 'relations of dependence': the relation of shopkeeper to big wholesaler, of peasant to landlord, of debtor to creditor, of proletarian to capitalist. This is one way in which social contract theory, with its postulate of free and equal individuals, distorts the reality that gave it birth – a form of distortion which it shares with the entire system of civil law (P, 190,164). But besides this it is distortive in ways peculiar to itself. The relationship of political authority, according to Pashukanis, is really in contradiction to the individual freedom and equality embodied, at least to some extent, in economic market trans-actions; hence the attempt to understand the former in terms of the latter must 'always appear as an ideological perversion of the facts'. Here 'ideological' means not only delusive (political authority is not, and cannot be, the outcome of agreement among free and equal individuals), but delusive in a way favourable to the bourgeoisie – for it distorts the reality of political power in capitalist society, which is the rule of the bourgeoisie, in its own interest, over the rest of society. In fact all government is class government, and social contract theory only obscures this fundamental fact (P, 149,182–3,187).

While Pashukanis's analysis is more general and wide-ranging than that of Macpherson, it is interesting to note a point on which they resemble yet differ from each other. For both these Marxist thinkers, the fundamental equality of individuals postulated in contract theory (or, for Macpherson, in that of Hobbes) reflects the economic reality of the capitalist market. But whereas for Macpherson it reflects a *real* equality in vulnerability to uncontrollable market forces, for Pashukanis it reflects the purely legal equality of men viewed as possessors of goods. Macpherson's version of the ideology thesis has already been discussed; it is now time to consider that of Pashukanis.

Pashukanis's argument raises many issues which are hard to treat adequately in the space available. One difficulty stems from his orthodox Marxist view, noted above, that all government is class government. If this were so, it would follow that *any* justification of government whatsoever (not just social contract theory) would be delusive and presumably ideological, even if (like contract theory much more often than not) it is concerned to place limits on government authority. The underlying premise here – that one may seriously envisage a society so ideally structured in respect of its economic base (in a word, communism) that no political authority is necessary (P, 156) – is one that many find hard to swallow. However, even if we reject it, it still remains open to investigation whether the (limited) justification of authority offered by contract theory is ideological in the ways claimed by Pashukanis.

One consideration that may make us reluctant to accept that claim arises from the Marxist concept of ideology that Pashukanis uses – namely the notion that an ideology *both* reflects *and* distorts the underlying economic reality. This looks suspiciously like trying to have things both ways – if a theory matches contemporary economic reality it is by that token ideological, if it contradicts it, it is ideological by that token too. Here it seems necessary to distinguish, more sharply than did Pashukanis himself, between law and political philosophy. Law is a social institution, not a theory; as such it is likely (bound?) to be functionally related to other social institutions such as the economy, indeed may be designed to fit them, but it cannot in the relevant sense reflect or contradict them – it cannot, strictly, be ideological. Political philosophy is a different matter; as theory, it may in principle be ideological in the Marxist sense. If we consider social contract theory, however, we find that, on Pashukanis's account, its premises do *not* correspond to the underlying socio-economic reality of capitalism, but in fact contradict them; for it postulates the natural freedom and equality of all individuals, whereas the socio-economic reality of capitalism is (says Pashukanis) inequality and dependence of one class on another. But this is *not* to say that those postulates of the theory *distort* that reality – for the theory does not offer any description of social reality, but is *prescriptive*. If, then, social contract theory is a prescriptive theory whose basic postulates contradict the real social relations of capitalism, it is very hard to see how capitalism could be the source of these basic postulates of the theory, or how these postulates could entail a justification of capitalist society, or a defence of the interests of the bourgeoisie. In fact, the great variety of contract theories shows that the basic postulates of the theory do not entail defence of any particular system – and in the case of Rousseau, in particular, led to a passionate attack on the status quo in the name of social equality (see above, pp.74–83). As for the *source* of the contractarian postulates of the natural freedom and equality of all men, it is indeed obvious from this study that they long antedate the rise of capitalism, and derive (as Macpherson indeed recognised) from a long tradition of Christian and Stoic speculation. From the standpoint of the theory of ideology it is particularly interesting that these ideas arose, in the ancient world, in startling and self-conscious contradiction to the contemporary social and economic reality (in which, for example, slavery was normal).

To say all this is not to deny that there is some affinity between the individualistic premises of 'classical' social contract theory, and the individualism of a market economy that operates through contracts. But the causal relations between them are likely to be more complicated than those that Pashukanis seems to propose. Quite likely, *both* are to a greater or lesser degree the heirs of that Christian individualism and Stoic-derived tradition of Roman law which we have briefly surveyed in an earlier chapter (see pp.23–4 above). Both of these currents of thought bequeathed to the sixteenth and later centuries, not only the conceptions of natural human equality and liberty, but also a concern with contracts (or, in the Christian case, covenants). The importance of Calvinism, with its stress on covenant theology, in the genesis of the classical phase of social contract theory, should not be forgotten (cf. pp.28, 32–6 above). None the less, it is not impossible that the growth of a contract-based market economy could have strengthened a (partly independent) tendency of political philosophers to think in terms of contract-legitimated political authority. To that extent Pashukanis's analysis may contain a partial truth. Undeniably, capitalism *is* an individualistic economic system, and the 'classic' social contract *is* an individualistic political theory. This, however, is a resemblance of a rather general kind; it certainly does not follow that, if capitalism is to be repudiated, social contract theory therefore must be too. Whether the individualism of contract theory is a strength or a weakness remains an open question; certainly there is no need to agree with Pashukanis that 'the category, subject of rights [in application to individuals], is in reality an abstraction from acts of exchange in the market' (P, 166). For the category, 'subject of rights' is not a purely legal one, as Pashukanis explicitly recognised. It is also a moral one, and as such was analysed, and repudiated, by him, in terms similar to those he applied to law. Thus: 'Man as a moral subject ... is no more than a condition of exchange according to the [capitalist] law of value'; hence 'the moral law must reveal itself as a rule of intercourse of commodity producers ... The basic concepts of morality have therefore no meaning of any kind if they are dissociated from commodity-producing [that is, capitalist] society' (P, 194–7). To read these words of Pashukanis is a somewhat chilling experience, in view of the fact that he himself was to perish, in 1937, in Stalin's terror – that orgy of lawlessness and amorality.

The tragic fate of Pashukanis may suggest that his diagnosis of law and morality as nothing but bourgeois ideologies was, after all, faulty. But let us return to social contract theory. Just now, the question of whether the individualism inherent in 'classic' contract theory is admirable or not was left open. I shall now consider a recent argument that strongly suggests that it is not. It is due to David Gauthier, and is to be found in an article whose title recalls that of this section of the present book: 'The Social Contract as Ideology'. Though Gauthier is no Marxist, it will become evident that his arguments have much in common with those of Pashukanis and Macpherson.

In brief, Gauthier's paper propounds two theses: the first is that 'contractarianism' (or, as he sometimes puts it, 'radical contractarianism') is central to the ideology of modern western society (Gauthier, 1977, pp.130–3,135). For Gauthier, the term 'ideology' does not have the pejorative connotations that it carries in Marxist theory; his first thesis is simply the claim that, more and more, (radical) contractualism constitutes our manner of conceiving human society. However, according to Gauthier's second thesis, the contractual ideology is actually incompatible with any stable social order at all – 'is, from a practical point of view, bankrupt, and ... will destroy us if we remain its adherents' (ibid., pp.160–4). From these two theses it follows that the contractualist ideology must be incoherent – it purports to be a way of understanding social order, yet destroys social order. It is, then, profoundly mistaken in theory and potentially disastrous in practice. But what exactly is this (radical) contractual ideology? Gauthier defines it as the view that human beings are by nature non-social, and that all their social intercourse is therefore instrumental – not good in itself, but good only in so far as it enables individuals better to forward their own (pre-social) purposes. All social institutions, therefore, are to be understood, and judged, as if they were the embodiment of (hypothetical) contracts made by such individuals; they must have a contractual rationale. However, since we are at the moment concerned only with institutions of political authority (as Gauthier partly is too), we may for our purposes take his contractarian ideology to refer to the theory that the rationale of such authority is a (hypothetical) contract between non-social individuals, that is, individuals for whom social relations have no intrinsic but only instrumental value.

According to Gauthier, a certain conception of human nature – of human motivation – is part and parcel of the contractual ideology, and one which is not adequately characterised as merely individualist. For social order enforced by political authority to be worthwhile to non-social individuals, Gauthier argues, these individuals must primarily or solely value goods of a certain kind: goods which (a) can be increased in quantity by social co-operation – making social order desirable – but which (b) give rise to conflicts between them over *distribution* of the goods available – making coercive authority necessary. In brief, they must primarily value 'economic' goods, and desire more and more of them. The contractarian ideology 'relies on the view that human activity is basically appropriative' (ibid., pp.141–7). To use terminology made familiar by C. B. Macpherson, social contract ideology assumes that men are not just individualists, but 'possessive individualists'. It sees the whole of society as being like an economic market.

Gauthier's main thesis is that this contractualist ideology is destructive of all social order – that the more and the more widely actual human motivation comes to match the ideology (as is increasingly the case), the more imminent is a collapse into 'chaos' (ibid., p.163). The trouble is that the maintenance of order among 'appropriative' individuals depends on their keeping their contracts; or, in the hypothetical mode, obeying institutions whose 'rationale' is contractual, including political authority. It depends on their restraining their 'appropriative' appetites. This, Gauthier argues, they cannot do; to do so would be to contradict the very 'nature' that underlies contractual ideology in the first place.

Gauthier's argument here is somewhat reminiscent of the well-known problem of collective goods, but does not in the end rely on it. Briefly, a collective good is a good valued by all members of a collectivity, which can be provided only in 'non-exclusive' form (that is, if available at all, it is available to all members of the collectivity). Provision of goods usually requires resources or involves costs (there being no such thing as a free lunch); but it may perfectly well be the case that the costs of a collective good could be divided up among the collectivity in such a way that every member would benefit overall from its provision. In that case, it is in the interest of all that the good be provided, with the appropriate division of costs; it would apparently be in the interest of all to sign a contract to contribute to providing the good in this way.

Or would it? If the collectivity is a large one, and the individual members are motivated purely by self-interest, there arises the notorious temptation to be a 'free rider'. For the contribution required of an individual may be negligibly tiny in relation to the total cost of the collective good, though significant to him. Why then make it? For, by hypothesis, the loss of this contribution makes no significant difference to the provision of the collective good which, by definition, if provided at all will be available to him. In that case, a purely self-interested individual has no good reason to contribute to the provision of a collective good. Hence it follows that a collectivity of self-interested persons cannot (in such cases) provide itself with collective goods – to the detriment of every individual member. They might indeed be prepared to sign a contract specifying the terms of their various contributions, but they would not – or not voluntarily – keep their contracts.

A standard example of a collective good is national defence, and the analysis just rehearsed can be cited as justification of a system of *taxation* for the purpose of this defence (or any other collective good). Taxation is coercion by the state in order to force individuals to make contributions, which can be used to provide collective goods. Such coercion is thus (or can be) in the interest of the coerced, who (uncoerced) would collectively act contrary to their collective interest. There is here a rather clear parallel with the social contract theory of political authority (especially that of Hobbes). In this case, the collective good in question is social peace, which (it is argued) can only be achieved by a central coercive authority; the 'contribution' required from each individual is abstention from aggression in cases where he could reap an immediate benefit therefrom. According to social contract theory, this abstention will not, given human nature, be sufficiently forthcoming on a purely voluntary basis, and so it is in the interests of everyone to accept an authority that enforces it.

There is, however, still a problem. On the assumptions of the argument so far, the self-interested individual, while favouring a coercive authority to enforce the law, will wish it to be successful in relation to everyone except himself. He is motivated to break the law whenever he expects to gain thereby; and restrained from such breach only if he expects to be punished for it. The 'free rider' problem, in other words, has not disappeared. If individuals are like this, it is doubtful if the state can be effective – can even survive. As Gauthier puts it: 'what real men and women who believe the [contractualist] ideology need to keep them from the war of all against all is . . . the Hobbist sovereign, and he is not available' (ibid., p.163). In other words, they had better not act on this ideology; they had better be motivated by such *social* motives as love and patriotism, and by internalised moral restraints.

Gauthier's analysis of the predicament of believers in the contractualist ideology differs somewhat from the standard exposition of the problem of collective goods. In the latter, the problem stems from the implications of the rational pursuit of individual self-interest. For a self-interested individual it is simply irrational to make his contribution to the provision of the good; for he is faced with two possibilities, either that the good is provided (because enough others contribute), or that it is not provided (because they do not). Either way he does better to contribute nothing, for (by hypothesis) his contribution is a significant cost to him, but makes no significant difference to the availability of the collective good. Individual rationality leads to collective irrationality. Somewhat surprisingly, Gauthier does not accept this argument, but claims that purely self-interested individuals, aware of this problem, would if rational see that they should abstain from maximising self-interest on every occasion and instead accept the necessary limiting conventions (or hypothetical contracts). However, he claims that the radically appropriative individuals assumed by contractualist ideology are simply unable to do so. Psychologically they *cannot* accept the necessary restraints (ibid., pp.154–7; 160).

This is a powerful indictment indeed, and as a diagnosis of the trend of modern society it may seem uncomfortably close to the mark. But should we really attribute our problems of social disorganisation to contract theory? I believe that Gauthier's argument goes too fast, and puts the blame in the wrong place. Crucial to it is the link he postulates between contractualism and 'appropriative' human nature; and on this crucial point he equivocates. The contractarian, he writes, 'relies on the view that human activity is basically appropriative', and reason cannot overcome the appropriative motivations 'which, on the contractarian view, direct our actions'. Yet (almost in an aside) Gauthier admits that contractualism does not *necessarily* entail the appropriative view of human psychology: 'I have not shown that no alternative account of human activity would afford nonsocial individuals with a rationale for a social contract' (ibid., pp.141, 160,149). And this is just the point; for in my view it is unlimited appropriativeness rather than contractualism that threatens social order.

Gauthier's onslaught on the social contract ideology has one slightly curious feature, namely, that while he discusses such prominent contractarian philosophers as Locke, Rousseau and Rawls, none of these are actually considered to be exponents of the ideology. Ultimately there is for Gauthier only one philosophical spokesman of 'radical' contractualism – Hobbes (ibid., pp.134–5, 139). Only Hobbes, that is, demands a contractual rationale for *all* social relations, institutions and duties. His reason, according to Gauthier's argument, is that he sees human nature as infinitely appropriative. Clearly Gauthier is here (as he freely acknowledges) much indebted to Macpherson's analysis; but I believe his argument is faulty. That argument, remember, is that naturally non-social individuals value coercively enforced social order only in so far as they value goods whose supply is increased by social co-operation, but over whose distribution conflict will arise among them – namely, economic goods. Hobbes's argument, however, is that naturally non-social individuals value the good of *peace*, or rather more basically the good of *life*, which is threatened by man's natural lust for power and glory and thus must be preserved by state coercion – a quite different story and one which is perfectly coherent. Infinite appropriativeness is therefore not necessary to Hobbes's argument, which is, in a general sense, perfectly in line with the entire tradition of social contract theory.

Gauthier's onslaught seems to me to exemplify a more general kind of mis-diagnosis of social contract theory – namely, that it is, so to speak, an apotheosis of selfishness. It is true that the theory makes some appeal to self-interest, but there is much more to it than that; equally, it is an appeal to moral obligation. What I earlier called the 'standard' form of the theory – which postulates adhesion to the contract as an actual event – appeals to the moral obligation to keep one's promises (and this, I have argued, applies to Hobbes as much as to his predecessors) (see above, p.58). The argument of 'standard' contract theory is, roughly, that one has a *moral* obligation to do what one must, *in relevant circumstances*, have promised to do, out of self-interest. This is by no means to say that one should or may always act selfishly, indeed it implies the contrary. Nor should it be forgotten that a social contract is not just a promise made for self-interested reasons – it is a promise that equally recognises the interests of the other parties to the contract. It promotes the interest, not of this or that individual, but of all. This, of course, is individualism, but it is not the apotheosis of selfishness.

Reformulation of social contract theory in the hypothetical mode alters the picture in details, but not in essentials. It is true that there can then no longer be any reliance on the moral obligation to keep promises; rather, the obligation postulated is to accept, support or obey institutions that are in one's interest, as well as in the interests of all others affected. Thus interpreted, Hobbes's argument is that there is an (almost absolute) *moral* obligation to obey the sovereign, because it is on balance in one's interest (and in everyone's interest) to be ruled by a nearly absolute sovereign: the argument is *not* that *obedience* to the sovereign is always in one's own selfish interest, which would be manifestly absurd. Admittedly, Hobbes's version of social contract theory is problematic, precisely because he does appear to postulate (though this has been disputed by some commentators) that all human action is selfishly motivated. It then becomes dubious whether such purely selfish individuals are *capable* of adhering to the moral obligation that Hobbes prescribes to them (cf. Gauthier above). But the important point is that Hobbes is in this respect *untypical* of social contract theory; that, indeed, the postulate of purely selfish human nature, far from being congruent with contract theory, threatens to undermine it.

It is worth looking further into the morality of contract. As explained in the opening chapter, the layman's conception of a contract, which is also that of standard social contract theory, is of a reciprocal, conditional exchange of promises. Each party promises something to the other(s), on condition that the other(s) fulfil(s) his/their promise. It follows that the morality of contracts is not simply a moral obligation to keep one's promise, though it is partly that. It is not very likely that a contract could be fulfilled by each of the parties performing their undertakings at the very same instant. In other words, contracts typically call either for a *succession* of actions, such that one party must perform first, or else for some *continuing* performance by the several parties (as Hobbes puts it, they involve covenants). The social contract, construed literally, falls in the latter category. It follows that, if a contract is effective, the individual contractor may (in the latter case, will) find himself in a situation where his fellow-contractor(s) have already fulfilled his/their contractual undertaking, in whole or in part. This situation, arguably, gives rise to a moral obligation over and above the obligation to keep one's promise – roughly, an obligation to *reciprocate* the contractual benefit one has received. This is an obligation which does not apply to someone who undertakes to be the first performer in a contract – to supply goods on credit, for example. But the purchaser to whom goods have been supplied in accordance with such a contract of credit has a moral obligation, not just to keep his promise to pay, but to pay *for what he has received* – a consideration which considerably strengthens his moral obligation. This obligation to reciprocate benefit is not a matter of self-interest, but is an obligation to give due respect to the interests of others. So far as the social contract is concerned, a similar argument is in principle applicable: the obligation to which it gives rise is not just an obligation to keep one's promise, but (if others have kept and are keeping their part of the contract) also an obligation to reciprocate the benefit by respecting their security, rights or whatever (the specifics vary, of course, according to the particular contract theory). Now, of course, we have admitted that the social contract is a fiction, and can at best be considered as a hypothetical concept from which to deduce political authority and its limits. Obligation to keep one's promise cannot survive reformulation of contract theory into the hypothetical mode; but the obligation to reciprocate benefit *can* do so, since one may perfectly well have received, in reality, the benefits stipulated in a contract that is merely hypothetical. Equally, one may not have received them; and this would be a ground for *denying* obligation.

The above argument about the morality of (social) contract seems to me rather similar to an idea put forward by H. L. A. Hart in his famous article 'Are there any Natural Rights?' Hart there suggests that political obligation is a kind of obligation arising from 'what may be termed mutuality of restrictions'. As Hart explains,

'when a number of persons conduct any joint enterprise according to rules and thus restrict their liberty, those who have submitted to those restrictions when required have a right to a similar submission from those who have benefited by their submission.

The rules may provide that officials should have authority to enforce obedience and make further rules, and this will create a structure of legal rights and duties.'

The moral obligation to obey such rules – political obligation – is owed to 'the co-operating members of the society' (Hart, 1967, pp.61–2) and is thus (though Hart does not use quite this language) an obligation to reciprocate benefit. Commenting on social contract theory, Hart remarks that it confuses obligation arising from 'mutuality of restrictions' with obligations arising from acts of promising (ibid., p.63). This is correct in so far as the social contract is construed literally; but if it is reformulated in the hypothetical mode, the obligation derivable from such a (hypothetical) contract appears to be, at least in part, an obligation to reciprocate benefit, by accepting restrictions on one's freedom, and to this extent similar to Hart's conception of political obligation. It is interesting in this connection that certain legal systems have recognised the doctrine of 'quasi-contract', which (according to a recent *Dictionary of Political Thought*) they deemed to exist whenever mutual interaction among persons was 'voluntary, and accompanied by manifest and intended advantages to the participants', thus giving rise to 'quasi-contractual' obligation (Scruton, 1982). Presumably this obligation was to reciprocate the benefit received from participation in the interaction. Of course, the state is not a voluntary form of interaction, but it is precisely the aim of social contract theory to show what advantages to individuals could be derived from it, and to deduce political obligation from that. Such obligation is not too different from the 'quasi-contractual' obligation just described.

In summary, so far as the issue of self-interest is concerned, social contract theory occupies what might be called a middle-of-the-road position. Up to a point, it appeals to the self-interest of the individual (and certainly does not call for self-abnegation), in so far as self-interest is assumed to be the motive for contracting. But the standard of legitimacy that it proposes is not the self-interest of any individual, but rather a (hypothetical) contract that promotes or reconciles the interests of *all* concerned. Thus the theory appeals not only to self-interest, but also to a due concern for the interests of one's fellows. It seeks to balance the equally legitimate interests of all. This fact, no doubt, accounts for the continuing popularity of the idea in present-day political discourse; and also makes intelligible the fact that the modern philosophical revival of contract theory has been, above all, as a theory of justice.

7 Contract Theory in Modern Times

The modern revival of social contract theory stems from the work of one man above all – the American philosopher, John Rawls. Rawls's seminal article, 'Justice as Fairness', appeared in 1958, was elaborated and modified in several further papers, and led up to his monumental book, *A Theory of Justice*, published in 1971. Since then innumerable critics have discussed Rawls's theory, and Rawls himself has continued to elaborate and modify it, a process still going on at the time of writing. It is no exaggeration to say that Rawls's theory presently dominates the field of political philosophy.

However, before going on to a discussion of Rawls's theory, it will be convenient first to consider another well-known work, which in fact pre-dated Rawls's book, and which explicitly, if less emphatically than Rawls, aligned itself with the social contract tradition. This is *The Calculus of Consent*, by James Buchanan and Gordon Tullock, first published in 1962. These authors also are American: unlike Rawls, however, they are by training not philosophers but economists, and they describe their enterprise as an attempt 'to derive a theory of collective choice that is in some respects analogous to the orthodox economic theory of markets'. Their book, therefore, belongs to the literature of collective choice and takes its inspiration from economic theory, rather than from political philosophy. Nevertheless it is a contribution to the latter, and one which, as one of its two authors (Buchanan) notes in an Appendix, 'falls within . . . the contractarian tradition', and has an unmistakable affinity with 'the contract theory of the state' (B & T, 18,317–20).

Like virtually all modern contract theorists, Buchanan concedes that the social contract is not a valid account of the historical

123

origins of government or governments. Rather, his suggestion is that it can provide a *criterion* for *changes* in political institutions. Roughly speaking, the idea is to use a hypothetical social contract as a standard for judging, and altering, these institutions. In line with the social contract tradition, the standard is what would be agreed by rational, self-interested individuals (or, in the economic jargon favoured by Buchanan and Tullock, utility-maximisers);[1] in other words, it is to be deduced from what the authors call a 'generalized economic theory of constitutions' (B & T, 63). This focus on political constitutions makes Buchanan and Tullock, in one way, more akin to their contractarian predecessors than Rawls, whose prime concern is social justice.

The starting-point for the development of Buchanan and Tullock's 'theory of constitutions' is what they call 'a situation characterized by no collective action'. 'No collective action' means no state – it is, in other words, equivalent to what in traditional contract theory was called the state of nature. Then, the theorists pose the question, 'When will a society composed of free and rational utility-maximizing individuals choose to undertake action collectively rather than privately?' (B & T, 43–4). That is, what areas of their life would such individuals agree to subject to collective regulation by the state? and on what terms? (what constitution would they accept?) In deducing their answer to these questions, Buchanan and Tullock make a crucial assumption: 'that the individual is *uncertain* as to what his own precise role will be in any one of the whole chain of later collective choices that will actually have to be made' (B & T, 78). In considering constitutional questions, therefore, the utility-maximising individual is not motivated to favour rules that promote sectional interests – he has no reason to think he will gain by them. This assumption is clearly necessary to ensure that the individuals in the hypothetical state of nature will accept institutions 'generally advantageous to all individuals', and only such institutions. Clearly implicit here is the same assumption as characterises traditional social contract theory, namely, that the appropriate standard of legitimacy for political institutions is that they be in the interest of all subject to them, compared with the state of nature.

What areas of their life would such rational, utility-maximising individuals agree to subject to collective regulation, and on what conditions? Conceptualising the matter in economic terms,

Buchanan and Tullock postulate that each individual will accept collective regulation when he expects the *costs* imposed on him by such regulation to be less than the costs he incurs through total freedom. These latter costs (of non-collectivisation) may arise either from the harmful actions of others, or from the failure to achieve the potential benefits derivable from collective goods (for the problem of collective goods, see the discussion in the previous chapter, pp.115–17). Buchanan and Tullock are primarily concerned with the latter; as they say, they prefer to '"jump over" the minimal collectivization of activity' involved in defining and enforcing basic human and property rights. This, of course, is to 'jump over' a primary concern of traditional social contract theory. This is not to say that Buchanan and Tullock consider these matters unimportant; rather, they consider it to be obvious – so obvious as to be not worth discussing – that every individual would find enforcement of these rights advantageous. 'The interesting, and important, questions concern the possible collectivization of activities beyond this minimal step' (B & T, 46–7).

Buchanan and Tullock's way of considering these questions is not in terms of the areas of life to be 'collectivised', but rather of the *decision-making rules* to be adopted by the state. What, for example, can be said about the system of *majority* decision, that is (loosely speaking) democracy? According to them, not much can be said for it. From the standpoint of the rational, utility-maximising individual, any collective decision (enforceable decision of the state) has, potentially, costs and benefits. He favours such a decision only if he judges that the benefits exceed the costs. To ensure that only those collective decisions are taken that yield him a net benefit, one and only one decision-making rule suffices – the rule of unanimity. Otherwise put, the only decision-making rule that ensures that all collective decisions produce genuinely collective goods (and not goods for only some members of the collectivity) is the rule that decisions must be agreed unanimously (B & T, 62–8). (It is, of course, not enough that they merely be agreed – what is to be agreed is that they be *enforced*. That collective goods cannot be supplied without enforcement was explained above, pp. 115–16).

Now, the social contract is itself a model of unanimous agreement as a standard of legitimacy for political institutions; and so far it may look as if Buchanan and Tullock's economic contractualism

has done nothing but endorse the very principle on which contractualism itself rests. However, the story is not yet quite finished.
According to Buchanan and Tullock, the preferred collective
decision-making rule would always be the rule of unanimity, but
for one further factor, not yet considered – the costs of decision-
making itself. From this point of view, the unanimity rule looks
much less advantageous, since the difficulties of arriving at unanimous agreement – in terms of time, energy and similar resources
required, in other words the costs likely to be incurred – are
extremely high. Indeed, the higher the proportion of members of
the collectivity whose agreement is required to validate a collective
decision, the greater the bargaining costs involved in getting
agreement. On the other hand, the higher this proportion is – the
nearer the decision-making rule is to the rule of unanimity – the
less is the likelihood, from the point of view of the 'average'
individual, that the decisions will be disadvantageous to him.
Under the unanimity rule, the *content* of all collective decisions
will certainly be acceptable to every individual; but the costs of
the *process* of collective decision will be very high. The *optimum*
decision-making rule, therefore, is whatever minimises the sum of
these two kinds of costs of collective decisions (B & T, 68–76).
All that can be derived from this analysis is that, due to the costs
of decision-making itself, the optimum rule is something less than
a rule of unanimity. No more specific conclusion is to be reached.
In particular, the analysis fails to provide any special endorsement
of the democratic collective decision-making rule, the rule of
majority decision. Buchanan and Tullock emphasise this as an
important finding, albeit negative (B & T, 81).

The thesis of *The Calculus of Consent* has the interest of a
pioneering effort, but it is deeply flawed. However, its flaws are
highly illuminating in relation to social contract theory in general.
The obvious objection to the argument of Buchanan and Tullock
is this: their analysis considers the likelihood of an individual's
suffering disadvantageous collective action, given different rules
of collective decision, but not (or not adequately) the likelihood
of his suffering disadvantage due to collective *inaction*. This is a
separate matter from the bargaining costs that may arise from
difficulties in arriving at agreement sufficiently widespread to
generate a decision (decision-making costs). If an individual has
grounds to favour a given collective decision, but not everyone

has, then a rule of unanimity prevents him from realising the benefits of such a decision and in this sense imposes costs on him. True, such a person may be able to achieve a part of these benefits by making strategic concessions to his opponents, or by offering them other inducements of one sort or another. But the point is that such bribes and concessions are themselves definite *costs*, which are ill-conceptualised as merely costs of decision-making. Furthermore, anyone who favours collective action to alter a status quo from which others derive large benefits may simply not have the resources necessary to bring about in these ways the kind of changes he desires; the nearer the decision-making rule is to a rule of unanimity, the harder it is to change the status quo by collective action. Thus it would *not* be rational for a utility-maximiser to prefer, decision-making costs apart, a rule of unanimity. It is clear that, by considering the costs to the individual of collective action but not (or not adequately) of collective inaction, the analysis of Buchanan and Tullock loads the dice against the former. This is undoubtedly a consequence of the authors' predilection for the free market.

It is interesting to compare Buchanan and Tullock's analysis with that of another collective choice theorist, D. W. Rae, in an article entitled 'Decision-Rules and Individual Values in Constitutional Choice'.[2] Rae invites us to consider an individual member of a collective decision-making body. If E_A is the likelihood that he supports a proposal but it is not adopted, and E_B is the likelihood that he opposes a proposal but it is adopted, then the best decision-rule for each individual is that which minimises $E_A + E_B$. E_A, of course, increases as the decision-rule approaches unanimity, while with E_B the reverse holds. Given certain assumptions, similar to those made by Buchanan and Tullock about the utility-maximising individual, and neglecting some minor complications, Rae shows that the decision-rule which minimises $E_A + E_B$ for all individuals is simple majority rule.

Thus, the conclusion reached by Buchanan and Tullock about the preferred decision-rule from the standpoint of the rational, utility-maximising individual appears to be untenable. However, it should be noted that Rae's conclusion holds only for an individual who has, *a priori*, no more reason to expect to find himself in the minority than in the majority, or vice-versa; members of a permanent minority faction clearly have an interest in a decision rule closer to the unanimity rule. Thus, those individuals who succeed economically in a free market ('the rich') may well be a minority with an interest in preventing collective action (redistribution, etc.) in the economic field. By their relatively positive attitude to the unanimity rule, and their relatively negative attitude to the majority rule, Buchanan and Tullock would strengthen their position. To this there are two quite separate objections, one of which has already been stated, namely that the analysis, arbitrarily, does not treat the costs of collective action and collective inaction even-handedly. The other is that the analysis assumes that collective action should take place *only if it benefits everyone in the collectivity*. That appears to rule out, for example, deliberate economic redistribution by the state from rich to poor, in the interest of the latter only. It is obvious that this is a highly controversial position. Yet it finds a parallel in social contract theory itself. For, the rationale offered by that theory for the existence of the state (in whatever form favoured by the theorist) is that it is advantageous for everyone, compared with the state of nature. Buchanan and Tullock extend this rationale much further, in effect applying it not only to the existence of the state in general, but to every activity of the state. Their theory of constitutions is much more of a contract theory than they perhaps realise; that is, framed in terms rather of what is advantageous to everyone, than of what is advantageous to their 'average' utility-maximising citizen (once we admit the existence of different classes of individuals with opposed interests, the two cease to be equivalent). This prompts a doubt about social contract theory itself. If collective action by the state may be justified even though not beneficial to everyone, perhaps similarly the existence of the state might be justified even if not beneficial to everyone, compared with the state of nature. It may or may not be the case (despite Hobbes's trenchant denial) that in a condition of anarchic lawlessness some individuals could flourish, at the expense of others, more than they would flourish in one of state-dependent peace; but if it *is* the case, surely (and contrary to the fundamental assumptions of contract theory in many of its forms) the state would still be justified by its putative consequences of peace and order.

Interestingly, Buchanan (1975) has turned his attention to some of these matters in a more recent book, *The Limits of Liberty*, which addresses itself *inter alia* to issues that were 'jumped over' in *The Calculus of Consent*. However, it does not seem that Buchanan's approach in the newer book is any more satisfactory than in the one co-authored with Tullock. Indeed, his analysis almost seems designed to substantiate the analysis-cum-indictment of Gauthier (see above, pp.114–15), for he considers the social contract above all in terms of its effect on the production and distribution of economic goods. In true contractarian style, the analysis begins by postulating a state of nature, lacking any centralised enforcement of law. What might economic activity be like in such a state of nature? For simplicity, Buchanan analyses the interactions of just two individuals of different kinds, A and B (we might, though, just as well postulate two kinds of individual, A-type and B-type). A (or an A) is a better worker than B (or a B), but a worse fighter. A, therefore, can achieve more utility for himself through work than can B, but B can improve his utility (and hurt A) by seizing some of what A produces. The distribution of goods produced by this combination of working and fighting is called by Buchanan the 'natural' distribution. Buchanan shows, by means of a diagram of a kind standardly used by economists (which those interested can consult in the original), that both A and B can gain from a 'social contract' that outlaws fighting and seizure. The argument is essentially a simple one. Fighting is economically wasteful; its abandonment therefore leads to greater productivity, and the increased product can be divided between A and B so as to benefit both. However, for B (the relatively poor worker but good fighter) to benefit from peace, the 'social contract' would probably have to arrange for *peaceful* transfer of some of the product of A's work to B. Both types of persons, that is, could gain by having a state that protects individual property, acquired by economic activity, but at the same time redistributes some wealth from the economically successful (the rich) to the others, for example by means of a progressive income tax (Buchanan, 1975, pp.53–71).

What follows from this analysis? Buchanan eschews any definite prescription as to the proper distribution of wealth, but he nevertheless suggests that the acceptability of any existing distribution to rational individuals should depend on how it compares with what they could expect to achieve from a social contract made in a 'state of nature' – in other words, on whether and how much it improves, from their point of view, on the 'natural' distribution.

'This approach offers a means of evaluating social rules, legal structures, and property rights' (ibid., p.75). If (as appears to be the case) Buchanan is *recommending* this mode of evaluation, then the proposal seems both unhelpful and, more importantly, misguided. It is unhelpful, since no one can say what the 'natural' distribution would be. It is, more importantly, misguided, because there is nothing sacrosanct about the 'natural' distribution anyway. There is no good reason to take it as a baseline. The natural distribution is what would result from skill both in work *and* in fighting. Why should wealth acquired by fighting (and seizing the product of others) be considered equally legitimate with wealth acquired by work? In Buchanan's model, A (the good worker) was portrayed as still richer under the 'natural' distribution than B (the good fighter), despite the depredations of the latter. But suppose the contrary were the case, as it very probably would be? Why should we say that an acceptable distribution must respect the parties' capacity for depredation, and guarantee that they should receive no less than they could acquire thereby? Yet if that idea seems absurd, it is (as was suggested above) an absurdity that infects the entire tradition of social contract theory, which postulates as the standard of legitimacy that which improves the situation of all by comparison with the state of nature. At any rate, it would certainly be absurd (or at least invalid) to postulate this standard as a necessary, rather than a sufficient condition of legitimate authority. As for Buchanan, although he finds in *The Limits of Liberty* a new rationale for economic redistribution that was absent from *The Calculus of Consent*, he is clearly still in thrall to the notion that, to be morally acceptable, collective action must benefit everyone involved. And he gives this notion an extra ideological twist by his extraordinary suggestion, in *The Limits of Liberty*, that the status quo must be treated as 'contractually legitimate' and departures from it be renegotiated, in effect, contractually – that is, by unanimous or near-unanimous agreement, rather than normal democratic procedures (ibid., p.85).

John Rawls

The efforts of Buchanan and Tullock to revive social contract theory in a hypothetical form cannot be considered to be successful.

Nevertheless they are interesting and instructive. One of the interesting features of their theories is the attempt to combine contract theory with the modern theory of rational choice; and this is a feature shared by the most important modern version of social contract theory, that of John Rawls. In other respects, however, Rawls's theory is very different from theirs.

It is also different in some important ways from the earlier contractarian tradition. Most notably, Rawls does not focus his attention on political obligation and the legitimacy of political authority – though these are not excluded – but rather on the *justice* of social systems and social structures. Social justice, as defined by Rawls, requires that the basic structure of society conforms to just principles ('principles of justice'), principles which ensure 'the proper distribution of the benefits and burdens of social co-operation' and a proper assignment of basic rights and duties (RJ, 5). Rawls's enterprise is to use social contract theory to derive these principles of justice.

The development of Rawls's theory has gone through several phases, and is still not at an end. Nevertheless, we must meantime take the formulation in his major book, *A Theory of Justice* (1971), as the authoritative version. One feature of the theory, however, has not changed. In common with practically all modern theorists, Rawls does not conceive of the social contract as an actual historical event; rather he wishes to use the idea as an 'analytic construction' (Rawls, 1963, p.103). Broadly his idea is this. The problem of justice arises in society because individual members of society make competing claims to the advantages produced by social co-operation. But despite this competition, it is theoretically possible that all members of society should agree on principles to regulate the distribution of these advantages. Furthermore, such an (hypothetical) agreement or contract can be taken as specifying principles *of justice* subject to one very important condition – that it be made in a situation which is itself *fair* as between all the parties involved. This hypothetical fair situation is called by Rawls the 'original position'. Much of Rawls's theory is devoted to specifying the features necessary to a fair original position, and to deducing – in the manner of a thought-experiment – what principles would be agreed in it by all parties (RJ, 11–22).

Let us now look at how he does so. Since the point of postulating this social contract is to arrive at a resolution of *conflicting* claims, the contracting parties must first be assumed to act on the basis of self-interest, in this sense: each is concerned to protect, and indeed maximise, his capacity to pursue *his own* ends or purposes (however noble or unselfish in some sense these purposes may be). In this way, the original position reflects what Rawls calls 'the circumstances of justice'. Also, the contractors in the original position must be assumed to be *rational* in the sense of acting in ways best suited to achieving their ends – otherwise the assumption of self-interested motivation could not be appropriately translated into contractual behaviour. The agreement, in brief, must be one acceptable to rational, self-interested people (RJ, 126–30,142–3).

Thus far, Rawls's original position reflects the features of the human condition that cause the *problem* of social justice. But it obviously must also be designed in such a way as to afford a proper (or fair) resolution of the problem. This implies, Rawls suggests, that the contracting parties must all be equal. In the original position all have the same rights. Really, this only re-affirms what is already implicit in the idea of the social contract itself – for a contract requires the agreement of all parties equally. A more substantive sort of equality is also necessary: the contractors must be 'sufficiently equal in power and ability that ... none is able to dominate the others'. In Rawls's famous article, 'Justice as Fairness' (1964, p.138), this requirement was explicit. In *A Theory of Justice*, however, it is an implicit consequence of a new, wider, and (as we shall see) much more controversial feature, which Rawls calls the veil of ignorance: that is,

> 'no one knows his place in society, his class position or social status, ... his fortune in the distribution of natural assets and abilities, his intelligence, strength, and the like ... The parties do not [even] know their conception of the good or their special psychological propensities.' (RJ, 12)

In brief, the contractors in the original position are ignorant of any features which distinguish or might distinguish them from their fellows. The justification of this is that it deprives the contractors of any motive to favour principles designed to further some particular interests at the expense of others – which would be unjust. The veil of ignorance forces on the hypothetical Rawlsian contractors a kind of impartiality. The point of Rawls's veil of ignorance, then, is similar to that of the postulate of *uncertainty* in the social (or constitutional) contract of Buchanan and Tullock's *Calculus of Consent* – the contractors have to be uncertain how the provisions agreed will turn out to affect them.

Rawls's version of this may perhaps seem puzzling. How could people rationally pursue their self-interest in contracting, if they didn't know anything about their particular characteristics, including even their purposes (their 'conceptions of the good')? And has not Rawls, in forcing impartiality on his contractors, nullified the circumstances of justice – conflict between opposed interests – that his construction is supposed to reflect? These difficulties are only apparent. The problem of decision-making under conditions of uncertainty is a perfectly standard one in, for example, economic theory. Also, the contracting parties do not need to know what particular purposes they wish to pursue, because what is to be regulated by the principles chosen in Rawls's original position is the distribution of what he calls *primary social goods*. These are (a) generalised *means* that promote, or may promote, people's purposes, more or less regardless of what, in particular, they are; and which are (b) typically the objects of conflicting claims in social and political life. They are, more specifically, 'rights and liberties, powers and opportunities, income and wealth'. All rational self-interested persons are presumed to wish to have as much of these goods as possible; as rational, they are presumed to understand the nature of these goods, and to have sufficient knowledge of the nature of social life to appreciate the bearing of social arrangements on their distribution (RJ, 62). The choice problem of the original position, therefore, is simply this: to secure the agreement on regulatory social principles of all putative individual members of society, on the assumption that they know only that they *are* members of a society and what this entails, in particular, that their society is subject to the circumstances of justice, that is, to conflict over the distribution of social primary goods, of which each wishes to maximise his share.

Rawls's spelling-out of the nature of the original position is, in my view, extremely illuminating as to the more or less implicit assumptions of the whole contractarian tradition. In particular, the postulates of self-interest, rationality and equality make explicit what was sometimes only implicit in the classic formulations of the theory. Nevertheless, the Rawlsian version of the theory is in some respects markedly different from the earlier, and in particular, the 'classic' versions. This goes deeper than Rawls's embracing of an avowedly hypothetical contract, deeper even than the difference between a theory of justice and a theory of the legitimate political constitution. For Rawls's original position, the situation prescribed for his contract, is *not* a state of nature. Nothing, indeed, could be less natural than Rawls's veil of ignorance. This is prescribed by Rawls, not in the least because he thinks of it as natural, but because it seems to him necessary to make the original position *fair*. The original position is designed to be an initial state of fairness, not a state of nature. The fundamental moral principle of Rawls's entire theory is *not*, therefore, that men are obliged to keep their promises, nor that they are morally obliged to obey social institutions from which they benefit (and so would have an interest in agreeing to, if they did not exist); it is that they are morally obliged to accept regulatory social principles (and institutions that conform to these principles) which they would agree to in a fair 'original position', if they were self-interested and rational. They have that obligation (or, in Rawls's preferred terminology, that duty) because such principles and institutions will be just (RJ, 114–15).

One question that now arises is whether Rawls's theory is, in the terms I introduced in chapter 6 above, an *ideal* or a *hypothetical* contract theory. This is a question of some importance if, as I have argued, in *ideal* contract theory (in the style of Kant) the contract is in fact superfluous, whereas in *hypothetical* contract theory (or contract theory hypothetically understood) it is not. The question is not easy to answer. I am inclined to say that, as a matter of fact, Rawls's contract theory is not straightforwardly one or the other. The contract he postulates is not the one that would be made by ideally moral beings. Nor is it the one that would be made by typical human beings in a hypothetical but quite easily imaginable and even possible situation, such as the state of nature. Rather, it is the contract that would be made by beings with reasonably realistic (and certainly non-ideal) *motivations*, in a situation that is quite unreal and, if not unimaginable, presumably impossible of achievement – behind the 'veil of ignorance'. It is a contract made by more or less realistically motivated hypothetical individuals in an imaginary ideal (that is, fair) situation. It does, then, rely on inferences as to what pursuit of self-interest would make acceptable to all concerned, and in this respect is much closer than, say, Kant to the mainstream of social contract theory. For this reason, too, it seems to me that the use of the contract to derive Rawls's theory is *not* superfluous, though this accusation has often been made against him. We shall have to return to it later.

Nevertheless, the difference between Rawls's original position and a state of nature is extremely important. In 'classic' contract theory, the state of nature serves as a baseline, a point of comparison. The self-interest of the parties to the contract moves them to *escape* from the state of nature, which is the situation they are in (actually or hypothetically) when they contract. They contract to move to a situation better than the state of nature. None of this applies to Rawls's original position, which is not an unsatisfactory state of affairs from which the contractors wish to escape, or on which they wish to improve. It seems, indeed, as if Rawls has set himself a task more difficult than did the older contract theorists; for while the latter concerned themselves only with how to improve on the state of nature, to solve some problems inherent in it, however severe, Rawls's contractors are faced with a problem of maximisation or optimisation – they have to choose the *best* outcome, from the viewpoint of their self-interest, given the constraints inherent in the ideally fair contractual situation. But actually, Rawls's task is not more difficult than that of the older theorists, and for two reasons. First, Rawls has simplified his problem by means of the veil of ignorance, which has the consequence that all his contractors are in effect identical, so that what is best for one is best for all (RJ, 139). Second, because the older theorists did not use any such concept, they are in fact, despite possible appearances to the contrary, faced with the problem that Rawls has made manageable – that of optimisation. If persons are to move out of the state of nature, *to what* should they move? Perhaps they could agree to anything that improves on the state of nature for them all, but why stop there? If some further state of affairs would be better still for some, they presumably prefer that – or rather they prefer whatever is best of all for them. But in fact no state of affairs can be best for everyone (if there are known conflicts of interest between them), while many possible states of affairs may be better for all than the state of nature. Which one to choose, then? The apparatus of traditional contract theory does not provide any way to decide, and this, I suggest, is one major reason why the different contract theorists proposed such very different contract theories. Viewed in this light (as well as others mentioned above – cf. pp.103–4,105,128) the use of the state of nature as a baseline or starting-point appears as a weakness of traditional social contract theory, and it will correspondingly seem that it is a strength of Rawls's theory that he dispenses with it. This is not to say, though, that Rawls's 'analytic construction' does not have problems of its own.

The fundamental premise of Rawls's theory, then, is that principles which our self-interest would lead us to agree to as the terms of a contract made in an ideally fair situation, are just; and that therefore such principles are morally obligatory for us. The first deduction from this premise is what Rawls calls a general conception of justice (it is really a general principle of justice), which addresses itself to the question of equality and inequality of distribution. Under what conditions if any would unequal distribution of primary social goods be favoured by a rational, self-interested Rawlsian contractor? Rawls's answer is, on condition that he gains from the inequality, is made better off by the inequality than by equality. But, because of the veil of ignorance and the uncertainty it creates, the Rawlsian contractor can be sure of gaining from inequality only if *all* do so. This yields the general conception or principle of justice. All social primary goods 'are to be distributed equally unless an unequal distribution of any, or all, of these values is to everyone's advantage', by comparison with an equal distribution (RJ, 62). More precisely, an unequal distribution is just if and only if it is to everyone's advantage compared with a *more* equal distribution (for if it is not, there is some *degree* of inequality not to everyone's advantage, and hence not acceptable to a Rawlsian contractor). Another way to put this stipulation is as follows: unequal distribution is just if it improves the position of those with the smallest share, compared with (greater) equality. Indeed, since a Rawlsian contractor behind the veil of ignorance must envisage the possibility that he may be among those with the smallest share, he must (Rawls argues) want to maximise the benefits accruing to the possessors of the smallest share of social primary goods. In so far, therefore, as inequality of distribution affects the benefits accruing to this worst-off group (whether it increases or decreases them), such inequality should ideally be set at the level that maximises these benefits (RJ, 150–51). The degree of inequality that optimises the worst-off social position is called by Rawls the 'best just' or 'perfectly just' distribution. Any lesser degree of inequality that still improves this position compared with (greater) equality is still just, though inferior to the best just distribution (RJ, 78–9).

All of this leaves completely open whether any inequality whatever can actually be considered just. However, it is fairly obvious that Rawls would not have taken the trouble to specify so carefully the terms of just inequality unless he believed that there was such a thing. In effect, then, the deduction of a general conception of justice from the original position is a deduction of justified inequality from the standpoint of an original equality. The transition from original equality to justified inequality is effected by the postulate of rational self-interest behind a veil of ignorance. The nature of the transition will perhaps become clearer as we move on to the second stage of Rawls's deduction, the special conception of justice.

In Rawls's general conception of justice (above), no distinction is made among the various social primary goods. Thus, it pronounces just an inequality in the distribution of rights and liberties, for example, so long as this produces sufficient extra economic benefits, say, for those with fewer rights or liberties. But Rawls is not happy to leave his theory at this point – hence his special conception of justice. The distinction between the two conceptions of justice rests, in essence, on a distinction between two kinds of society (or levels of social development) – societies which have, and those which have not, achieved a level of civilisation such that it is possible to establish, in a meaningful way, certain basic liberties for all. Roughly, Rawls thinks of this as a consequence of the degree of economic development. Thus, in a society where everyone is or can be sufficiently well-off economically to make the basic liberties meaningful, it would, Rawls argues, be against one's interest to accept a curtailment of these liberties in return for further economic or other improvement, no matter how great. In other words, loss of basic liberties in such a case simply *cannot* benefit the losers (except perhaps by better securing *other* basic liberties) – or, as Rawls puts it, in these circumstances, basic liberties have *priority* over other social primary goods (RJ, 60–3, 151–2,542–5). These basic liberties are: 'political liberty (the right to vote and to be eligible for public office) together with freedom of speech and assembly; liberty of conscience and freedom of thought; freedom of the person along with the right to hold (personal) property; and freedom from arbitrary arrest and seizure as defined by the concept of the rule of law'. This list, Rawls says, is illustrative rather than definitive – and there are indications that he would wish to add to it, for example, freedom of association and the free choice of occupation (RJ, 61,310,328–9,272).

The priority of basic liberty is a part of the special conception of justice, which is applicable to sufficiently 'developed' societies, and expressed not in one principle, but two, as follows:

1. The basic liberties must be fully enjoyed by all equally (unless an unequal distribution of these liberties improves the total basic liberty of those who have less);
2. Social and economic inequalities are to be arranged so that they are both
   (a) to the greatest benefit of the least advantaged, and
   (b) such that advantaged positions are open to all under fair equality of opportunity (unless unequal opportunity improves the opportunities of those who have less).

The above is a condensed version of Rawls's own formulation of his special conception of justice (RJ, 302–3). In my opinion, however, it is rather clumsy and even misleading, and I shall shortly offer an (I hope) improved version. Rawls's reason for his own formulation, in the form of two principles, is apparently that he thinks of each one as applying to a different part of the social structure: (1) provides standards for the political constitution – essentially those of a liberal constitutional democracy; (2) regulates the organisation of the economy and the occupational structure (RJ, 198–9). But to me parts (a) and (b) of principle 2 are separate and best formulated quite separately, particular in view of the fact that 2(b) states, in its parenthesis, a priority for social and economic *opportunities* (opportunities, that is, to achieve desired social and economic positions) over the other social and economic goods such as income and wealth (though *not* over the basic liberties). Apparently, Rawls's rationale for this second priority is that human beings greatly enjoy the realisation and exercise of their capacities; hence it is rational, once a basic level of economic well-being has been achieved, to prefer to safeguard opportunities for such self-realisation rather than to become richer (RJ, 414,426–9). I therefore propose the following re-formulation of Rawls's special conception of justice:

1. The basic liberties must be fully enjoyed by all equally (unless an unequal distribution of these liberties improves the total basic liberty of those who have less);
2. There must be fair equality of opportunity for all to achieve desired social and economic positions (unless unequal opportunity either improves the opportunities of those with fewer opportunities, or improves their basic liberties);
3. Inequalities in other social and economic primary goods (income, wealth, power, authority) must be such as to benefit those who have less of them, indeed to benefit most those who have least of them.

In this formulation, the idea of Rawls's general conception of justice is applied *separately and successively* to three different classes of social primary goods, in the order of their priority as conceived by Rawls in a sufficiently developed society; the formulation of the respective principles expresses those priorities. Thus, only universal improvements in basic liberty can justify inequality of basic liberty; but inequalities in 'other social and economic primary goods' can be justified by universal improvements in any social primary goods. For example, inequalities in economic reward can be justified if they are so arranged as to provide incentives that increase social wealth, and the increased social wealth is used to benefit the relatively less well-off. Given the safeguarding of basic liberties and fair equality of opportunity, economic inequalities should be arranged so as to optimise the economic well-being of society's poorest class. This is Rawls's famous 'difference principle'.

Undoubtedly, Rawls's main interest, as a member of a wealthy society, is in the two (or three) principles of the special conception of justice. So far as political organisation is concerned, this conception prescribes, as the 'just constitution', a liberal representative democracy with the safeguarding of traditional civil rights; as for the economy, it prescribes a free market system (for the sake of efficiency and respect for the basic liberties), together with extensive redistribution by the government (to ensure that society's wealth is so distributed as to make the poorest group as rich as possible, in accordance with the difference principle). On the issue of private or public ownership of economic assets, Rawls declines to take sides. In brief, Rawls's version of a just society is a liberal welfare democracy (RJ, 201–84). And this, he argues, is derivable from contractarian premises: it conforms to principles that rational, self-interested persons would agree to, behind a veil of ignorance.

Discussion of Rawls's theory

As already mentioned, Rawls's theory of justice presently domi-nates the field of political philosophy. It has been the focus of a colossal volume of comment, much of it highly critical. Any thorough survey of objections to Rawls is here out of the question; I shall therefore confine myself to those which seem most germane to our general theme.

To open the discussion, I propose to broach three, somewhat connected, types of criticism that have been made of the Rawlsian theory. They are the following:

1. The theory is not genuinely a contract theory at all.
2. The role played by the contract in Rawls's theory is superfluous and dispensable.
3. Rawls manipulates his contractarian argument in an arbitrary and question-begging way.

Criticisms 2 and 3 are closely akin, in that both imply that Rawls's real arguments for the conclusions he favours do not genuinely derive from his contractarian premises. Criticism 1, on the other hand, asserts that these premises are not even genuinely contractar-ian.

Let us begin with the accusation that Rawls, despite all his enthusiasm for the contractarian tradition, has not succeeded in producing a social contract theory. Two connected features of Rawls's theory seem to give colour to this charge: that the original position in which the contract is postulated to occur is not a state of nature, and that the contractors operate behind a veil of ignorance. In an ordinary contract, we normally have parties who, in the light of their existing circumstances, and their particular interests and goals, come to an agreement on some joint mode of proceeding which all expect to bring about an improvement relative to the existing circumstances. 'Classic' social contract theory corresponds to this formula, with the state of nature functioning as the baseline situation in which, and in relation to which, individuals decide to contract. Again, an ordinary contract is normally a bargain, in which each party achieves an improvement on the status quo by offering like improvements to his partner(s) in return; each, that is, gives up something in return for what is to him a greater gain. But the Rawlsian original position is *not* a state of nature, nor is the Rawlsian contract envisaged (either by Rawls or by his hypothetical contractors) as an *improvement* on a state of nature or any other situation real or hypothetical. One feature of the ordinary contract, and of the classic social contract, is therefore lacking in Rawls's theory. Further, not only are Rawlsian contractors not bargaining their way from a worse situation to a better, but because of the veil of ignorance there can be no bargaining between them at all – the veil, designedly, deprives them of any basis for such bargaining, by making the interests of all parties, in effect, identical (RJ, 139). One critic of Rawls, Jean Hampton, has complained that a contract where bargaining is in principle impossible is no real contract at all (Hampton, 1980, pp.321–5). Another, Michael Sandel, charges that the veil of ignorance, by making all the contractors in effect identical, negates that *plurality* of different individuals, and their conflicting interests, that Rawls's contractarian premise is avowedly designed to reflect, and concludes that 'what goes on in the original position is [therefore] not a contract after all' (Sandel, 1982, pp.122–32).

I believe that these and similar criticisms of Rawls are not justified. To be sure, the Rawlsian contract differs from an ordinary contract and also from the contract of classic social contract theory. It does not, however, differ from the latter in respect of the absence of bargaining, of give and take. In principle, bargaining is doubtless possible in the state of nature; but the classic social contract theories never postulated it, and the reason is clear – if they had done so, they would have yielded no determinate conclusions. Rather, each theory simply posits its own conclusions as the 'obvious' outcome of the contract, presumably optimum for all contractors. Bargaining would be as fatal to classic social contract theory as to Rawls's. But Rawls improves on the classic theory by, unlike them, designing the premises of his argument so as to make the exclusion of bargaining intelligible. As for Sandel's charge that the deliberations of identical individuals (made identical by the veil of ignorance) cannot lead to a contract – that identical individuals are no genuine plurality of individuals – I believe that, though Sandel's is among the subtlest and most thought-provoking of the many critiques of Rawls, this part of it is simply wrong. Many identical individuals are still many individuals: they may still have conflicts of interest, all the more so if (as in Rawls's theory) part of their identity consists in a desire to maximise control over the same primary social goods, which are in limited supply. Hence a contract between identical individuals is no contradiction, even though all reason alike and easily reach the same conclusion. I therefore conclude that the contract that features in Rawls's theory, while in many ways unlike an ordinary contract and unlike the classical social contract, is still a genuine social contract.

But even if the contract postulated by Rawls is a genuine contract, it may still be superfluous, playing no real role, or at any rate no necessary role, in his argument. This charge against Rawls usually focuses on his original position. If the original position is not a state of nature – and is thus not a deduction from a supposed human nature, as in classic contract theory – how is it to be defined? Rawls explicitly seeks to define it in such a way as to be *fair* as between the parties; but fairness (unlike a state of nature) is a matter of *moral* judgements. Hence the original position both reflects certain moral judgements or principles, and is supposed to yield (via the contract) certain moral principles (the principles of justice). The charge against Rawls is that these two sets of moral principles are essentially the same, or that the former yield the latter directly, without any necessity for the interpolation of an original position or a contract. In the view of one critic, Rawls's argument from the original position is simply unnecessary (Honderich, 1975, pp.68–70), to another it is merely an expository device (Carr, 1975, pp.87–8), to a third it is necessarily and viciously circular: 'what one derives from the original position is wholly dependent on what one puts into it', and 'it is not possible to define the original position in such a way that it will yield a definite result from non-question-begging premises' (Browne, 1976, p.7). This brings us to our third criticism of Rawls – that he manipulates his contractarian argument in an arbitrary and question-begging way.

I believe these criticisms of Rawls's method are somewhat confused, though they are not baseless. They seem, in the first place, to ignore Rawls's own account of his procedure, namely, that he seeks to derive relatively strong (non-obvious, controversial) conclusions from relatively weak (widely accepted, uncontroversial) premises (RJ, 18). If the premises are indeed widely acceptable, and the derivation is sound, then the conclusions can be made widely acceptable also. The question now is whether the contractarian argument is essential to this derivation as Rawls presents it. I believe that it is. The only *moral* principle incorporated into the original position is the equality secured by the veil of ignorance; the moral principle embodied in Rawls's principles of justice is a specification of justified (and unjustified) *inequality*. The bridge leading from initial or hypothetical equality to a specification of justified inequality is the postulate of rational self-interest; that is, the rational self-interest of all concerned. This postulate is quite typical of the social contract tradition; and without it, Rawls would not be able to generate his conclusions. As stated above, his basic premise is that just principles are those that would be agreed by all concerned in a fair initial position, assuming they were rational and self-interested. This necessary premise is a contractarian premise.

However, to say this is by no means to acquit Rawls of the charge of question-begging or arbitrariness. Indeed, this – as we have seen – is a charge that can be brought against social contract theory quite generally, because of its reliance on unprovable and perhaps fundamentally illegitimate postulates of universal human nature. Rawls, like his predecessors, cannot get anything out of his contract theory without making some specific motivational assumptions about his contractors – that is, about the human race in general. But can such assumptions be sufficiently general not to be question-begging, and at the same time sufficiently specific to yield definite conclusions? Many issues arise here, and correspondingly many criticisms have been made of Rawls, which need to be disentangled. As we shall see, some are sound, and some are not.

I shall start with a criticism which, I believe, is unsound: that the Rawlsian contract (in an arbitrary, question-begging way) loads the dice in favour of liberal individualism, even of 'possessive individualism' (that is, capitalism). This criticism immediately reminds one of the similar criticism made of earlier social contract theories (see above, pp.105–15), so it at least suggests that Rawls's theory genuinely belongs to that genus. And, interestingly, as with the similar criticisms of the older theories, this objection (as we shall see below) bases itself on both of two, apparently opposite grounds – that the premises of Rawls's theory are too general, and that they are too particular.

We must be clear what this objection to Rawls amounts to. It is beyond any question that Rawls's theory of justice is – and is meant to be – a defence of liberal individualism. What is at issue is whether the contractarian premises which he uses to buttress this defence already beg the question. A number of critics have argued that they do, simply on the grounds that his contractors in the original position are postulated as being self-interested. This particular objection – which repeats a standard criticism of social contract theory generally – seems particularly ill-judged in relation to Rawls. For Rawls's theory is a theory of *justice*; and the problem of justice only arises, as Rawls points out, because of the claims of competing self-interests. The self-interest of Rawlsian contractors (unlike that of Hobbesian ones, for example) does not express the theorist's view of human nature, but of that *aspect* of human nature that gives rise to the problem of justice (RJ, 128–9). It thus turns out that social contract theory is especially suited to dealing with that problem: that, perhaps, is Rawls's major insight. Of course, if the 'circumstances of justice' do not obtain, there is no place for a theory of justice (and Rawls may conceivably be at fault in so far as he assumes that they do obtain, in all societies); but *as* a theory of justice, to the extent that such is relevant, no objection can be made to it on this score.

The charge of using question-begging individualist premises can be brought against Rawls in a subtler way, though ultimately, in my view, with no greater success. Thus C. B. Macpherson (whom we have already encountered in the previous chapter as a critic of contract theory) objects to the portrayal of the interests of the Rawlsian contractors as necessarily *conflicting*; this, he points out, need be so only if their desire for the primary social goods is *infinite*, whence he deduces that Rawls operates here with a bourgeois 'model of man' (Macpherson, 1973, pp.342, 345–6). Michael Sandel reaches a rather similar conclusion through a very different argument. Because Rawls seeks a completely *general* 'model of man' (to borrow Macpherson's phrase) his concept of the person is of a self quite detached from any particular aims or interests. This, Sandel complains, 'rules out the possibility that *common* purposes and ends' (emphasis added) could actually be constitutive of the selves of members of a community (and of that community). This exaltation of individual over common purposes is, to Sandel, the 'deeper sense' in which Rawls's premises are biased towards individualism (Sandel, 1982, pp.62–4). But, once again, common identities, common purposes, and absence of conflicting interests, however desirable, are simply irrelevant to a theory of justice. Rawls, to be sure, does use (not a bourgeois, but) an individualist 'model of man'. But justice is an individualist virtue.

Let us turn to another way in which the premises of Rawls's contract theory have been said to be question-begging, one which focuses on the idea of primary social goods. This idea is intended by Rawls to solve the 'human nature' problem that beset his contractarian predecessors; he can assume that all individuals want to have, indeed to maximise, these goods, without implying thereby that all have the same ultimate values or goals or 'conceptions of the good' – primary social goods are supposed to be generalised *means* to facilitate whatever goals one has. But are they? Joyce B. Hoy has complained (in an avowedly Hegelian spirit) that they are not: that they are historically specific, and inevitably so. Thus freedom is a peculiarly modern preoccupation, while wealth is far from being universally valued (several critics of Rawls have pointed to the phenomenon of the ascetic, for whom material wealth has negative value), and so on (Hoy, 1981, pp.411–13). How should we assess this objection?

I believe that it is of limited importance, so far as Rawls's *general* conception of justice is concerned. The general conception (see above, p.136) prescribes a distribution of primary social goods in a quite general way. Therefore, it is not strictly necessary for it to specify what these goods are. Rawls's list – liberties, wealth, and so on – can be taken as simply illustrative, and the following, generalised definition of a social primary good can be employed:

a social primary good is *any* good valued in a given society as a generalised means, the distribution of which is affected by social arrangements (and also gives rise to conflict between members of society). The general principle of Rawlsian justice would then simply be that in any society its primary social goods should be distributed equally unless an unequal distribution benefits all.

But the problem is much greater when we come to the two principles of Rawls's special conception of justice, which is, indeed, the main focus of his interest. Here it seems impossible to avoid talking about specific primary social goods; and the problem is compounded by Rawls's introduction of priority rules among them. Innumerable critics of Rawls have protested, for example, against the arbitrariness of his awarding top priority to basic liberties and bottom priority to economic goods (above whatever minimum is needed to make the basic liberties 'effective'). Rawls's contention is that this would be the evaluation of any rational self-interested person in the original position (that is, behind the veil of ignorance). Now, a case might be made for this priority for *some* of Rawls's basic liberties (for example, freedom of the person, or freedom from arbitrary arrest – arguably no tolerable life is possible without these), but scarcely for all. It may indeed be right to prefer freedom of conscience, freedom of speech, democratic rights and so on to greater wealth, but this is exactly what Rawls has to show. His contractarian premises do nothing in this direction. Like so many of his predecessors, he seems to attribute his own values to the contractors who, for theoretical purposes, represent mankind in general.

There is yet another problem, of a rather similar kind, and one which threatens both Rawls's 'conceptions' of justice, general and special. Specific primary social goods and priority orderings apart, these two conceptions have in common the requirement that inequalities must benefit all. To represent this requirement as the preference of a rational self-interested contractor behind the veil of ignorance appears, once again, to rest on a specific, but unavowed, motivational assumption; what is called, in the jargon of decison-theory, risk-averseness. The Rawlsian contractor is *uncertain* whereabouts he will find himself in the social structure, whose general shape his preference is to determine; therefore, Rawls appears to argue, his preference is determined by *fear* of finding himself in its lowest socio-economic class. Indeed, it would not be different if he were *certain* of finding himself in that class – so that the fate of all those in higher classes (to which he might after all belong) becomes in effect irrelevant. Once again, many critics of Rawls have complained of the arbitrariness of this argument, which is supposed to be a deduction from rational self-interest alone. Perhaps the best-known of these critics is J. C. Harsanyi,[3] who has used a rational-choice construction rather similar to Rawls's original position to argue for a kind of utilitarianism, or more specifically for social arrangements that maximise the average level of welfare in society, rather than the lowest level (as required by the Rawlsian principles). Harsanyi can plausibly claim that a rational chooser in the Rawlsian original position, having no reason to expect to occupy one social position rather than another, should pay attention to the average of *all* social positions. A Harsanyi society would be much *riskier* than a Rawlsian society, since in it nothing whatever is stipulated about the lowest level of welfare, or of primary social goods, which could quite easily be too low to support life. Nevertheless, Rawls's attempts to refute Harsanyi's deduction from their shared premises seem to me unsuccessful, at least without the extra assumption of risk-averseness on the part of the contractors. Indeed, the Rawlsian deduction appears to require their *total* risk-averseness. A lesser degree of risk-averseness could lead them to choose principles intermediate between those of Harsanyi and Rawls; that is, the stipulation of some 'social minimum' (in Rawls's terminology) but not the 'maximum minimum' (maximin) called for by the Rawlsian principles (RJ, 152–4).

None of this should be taken as suggesting that utilitarianism could be an adequate principle of justice – notoriously, it is not. Rather, it appears that Rawls's premises, in failing to exclude utilitarianism, are defective in some way. The fault, it seems, lies in the part played in his deduction by the notion of *choice under uncertainty*, which makes the outcome dependent on attitudes to risk, and therefore (unless the aversion of the chooser to risk is implausibly made total) permits a degree of 'riskiness' in the conclusions. Such conclusions, however, cannot do what Rawls needs, that is, safeguard those rights of individuals that justice requires. This, then, is the disadvantage of Rawls's veil of ignorance. If, on the other hand, he were to drop that feature of his original position, thus aligning himself more closely with traditional social contract theory, then all the latent problems of that theory would return to plague him; more precisely, the problem of finding a single optimum on which all contractors can agree, despite manifest differences between them in aims and circumstances. In traditional contract theory, this problem was not overt, perhaps not even noticed, but is apparent in the widely divergent conclusions reached by the various theorists. Rawls's more ambitious contractualism renders the problem apparent at once. As one of his most famous critics, Robert Nozick, has pointed out, there is no hope that the difference principle (or for that matter the Rawlsian general conception of justice as a whole) would be acceptable to all rational self-interested persons, once the veil of ignorance was removed (N, 192–7). The difference principle (designedly) makes the less well-endowed members of society better off, and makes the better endowed worse off, than they would be in a contractual system of completely free economic exchanges (that is, a market, without government intervention); therefore, it would not be acceptable to the better endowed as the terms of a social contract. To Nozick, precisely this makes the difference principle *unjust*; it violates *his* principle that individuals are entitled to keep whatever others freely transfer to them (N, 150–3, 160–3). To Nozick, Rawls's version of the social contract, paradoxically, violates the contractual principle on which the market is based. If this is true, it at least suggests that Rawls's theory is not a piece of bourgeois ideology; nevertheless, the problem of the indeterminacy of the theory, with or without a veil of ignorance, remains unresolved. To repeat: with the veil of ignorance, the outcome depends on apparently arbitrary assumptions about attitudes to risk; without it, it depends on an unpredictable process of bargaining between conflicting interests.

Whether this problem can be resolved is a vital question, to which I shall return. Before doing so, however, something more should be said about Nozick's rival theory of the state and justice, and its relation to social contract.

Nozick's theory

In brief, Nozick's project is a defence of the minimal state, which, roughly speaking, is a state that enforces the Lockean natural rights of life, liberty and property, and does nothing more. The project has two parts: a justification of the minimal state, and a refutation of the case for any more-than-minimal state, especially an economically redistributive state. The terms of Nozick's criticism of Rawls (cited above) might suggest that the basis for his argument is some kind of contractarianism, and indeed his theory does bear an interesting relation to the social contract tradition, in that the concept of the state of nature plays a major role in it, and contracts or agreements made in the state of nature bulk large. Nevertheless, Nozick dissociates himself from the social contract tradition (N, 132), and in my view he is right to do so (though not for the reason he himself gives).

Nozick's theory is like Locke's in many ways, but differs from it in others. Both theorists consider all individuals to have natural rights of life, liberty and property, as well as a 'secondary' natural right to enforce these primary natural rights. Both envisage individuals in a state of nature contracting to transfer the secondary natural right of enforcement to a larger association, for the sake of more efficient protection of the primary rights. But whereas for Locke this larger right-enforcing association is the state, whose authority is thus founded on the consent of all its subjects, in Nozick's version, individuals, in the first instance, contract with (one or more) *private* protective agencies, which offer the state-like function of protection as a commercial service (N, ix, 4–15). So far, so contractual – but Nozickian private protective agencies are not states, and exercise no political authority. The establishment of the latter, in Nozick's account, need have nothing to do with contract. Rather, he envisages that, in any given geographical area, there emerges one *dominant* protective association, whether through agreement between agencies or as a result of fighting between them (N, 15–17). But territorially dominant protective associations are still not yet states: it is possible that within their territories there are individuals who have chosen not to transfer their enforcement rights to the association, and so receive no protection of their natural rights from the association. Nozick, however, claims (in a complex argument that need not be reproduced here) that the dominant protective association would be entitled to *force* these 'independents' to transfer their enforcement rights to it, in return for protection (N, 22–5,54f.,101–19). If and when a dominant protective association thus claims and imposes a monopoly of law-enforcement, it becomes a state – a minimal state, exercising legitimate political authority.

What exactly is the point of Nozick's account? Certainly he does not imagine that states actually came or come into existence in the way described. In this sense the whole story is hypothetical, or rather an account of what *might* happen, starting from a hypothetical state of nature. But why should we be interested in the fact that this might happen (so, after all, might innumerable other things)? Nozick's answer, apparently, is that it demonstrates how a state can come into existence without any violation of the moral rights of any individual – so long as it is a minimal state (N, 114). The fighting between protective agencies that is part of the story is seen by Nozick as a regrettable outcome of differing interpretations of their respective clients' rights, but not as a breach of anyone's rights. Similarly the coercion of independents needed to complete the last lap to statehood is no breach of their rights – so long as the state established is a minimal state. On the other hand, coercive establishment (or imposition) of a state which is more-than-minimal – for example, engages in economic redistribution – violates rights and is illegitimate (N, 167–74).

But this means, in effect, that the entire story of protective agencies, and the contractual elements in the story, are redundant. If it is legitimate for a dominant protective agency to force a few independents into a minimal state, presumably it is just as legitimate for any person or group of persons, no matter how small a minority of the population of a territory, to do the same to the majority of its inhabitants. What difference can it make how many people are forced, or do the forcing, to a theorist like Nozick for whom individual rights are all? What can it matter whether the enforcers are or are not *already* a protective agency that has entered into commercial contracts? All that can matter is whether the state established is a legitimate state, that is, one which (for Nozick) enforces the individual natural rights and does nothing more. Against Nozick's theory the stricture, so often levelled unjustly at contract theories like Locke's, is in fact just – that the elaborate account of the state's origin is irrelevant, and all that really matters is what kind of state it is. For in social contract theory, even if the contract is hypothetical, the contractualist account addresses itself to showing what promotes the interest of all concerned; and it is precisely this that Nozick's account, because it allows coercion, fails to do. Hypothetical contract is of some interest; hypothetical coercion has none.

Despite all this, Nozick's theory entails some significant commitments of a contractarian kind. Coercion to establish a minimal state would be legitimate, coercive redistribution of wealth by the state (he holds) is not, because (or rather if) it robs individuals of what is rightfully theirs; and it is rightfully theirs if they acquired it, by means of a free contract or other agreement, from its previous rightful owner (N, 149–53). Now, Nozick does not contend that any existing economic distribution has resulted solely from such free contracts or other similar transactions; he admits that these distributions have been partly shaped by acts of violence and aggression in the past (N, 152, 231). So, by his criterion, neither existing distributions, nor the redistributions that states might enforce, are just (even though his entire animus is directed against state redistribution). What, then, is the just distribution? The answer must be – that distribution that *would* have come about purely as a result of free transactions, such as contracts. But this commits Nozick to a kind of hypothetical contractualism. It commits him to accept that, if there were any principle of distribution that would be agreed by all members of a society, that principle of distribution would be just. Nozick, as we saw, denies that they would accept the Rawlsian principles, and this is for him a decisive objection to Rawls's theory. But are there *any* principles which, one might plausibly argue, all would accept, or which it would be in the interests of all to accept? To this central problem of contract theory we may now return.

Conclusion on contractarian justice

It may seem, from our discussion to this point, that the problem is insoluble; and it must be admitted straight away that the difficulties, stemming from differences of interests, values and goals among different individuals and societies, are formidable. But the case may not be quite hopeless. In this section I shall investigate the possibilities of a less ambitious kind of social contract theory that, making a virtue of its modesty, seeks to sidestep the difficulties.

Let us look first at the issue that divides Nozick and Rawls, and at the same time at the problem of attributing arbitrary attitudes to risk to hypothetical contractors. Nozick, we know, objects to Rawls's difference principle on the ground that it would not be acceptable to the better endowed members of society; others object to it on the ground that, from behind the veil of ignorance, its acceptance requires (arbitrarily) a total aversion to risk. But now, we can use a suggestion by J. S. Coleman to make some headway against both these problems (Coleman, 1976, p.435; Coleman, 1977, pp.187f.; cf. also B & T, 192–3). Coleman points out that, even if the veil of ignorance is removed, it is quite likely that the members of a society could reach some agreement to establish a social minimum through state redistribution of wealth – or at least, that it would be in the interest of all to agree to do so. The point is that such a social minimum constitutes a system of social security, a kind of insurance policy against dire misfortune. Now, the kind of economic system favoured by Nozick is a free market system, which he (like many of its other champions, such as Hayek) supports precisely because it is *free*. But – as both Nozick and Hayek themselves stress – the concomitant of this freedom is unpredictability.[4] No one can be sure how things will work out. What Nozick calls 'endowment' is relative to market demand – skills no longer demanded cease to yield an income. He who is rich to-day may lose his source of wealth to-morrow, in a free market regime – quite apart from the fact that accident or injury may deprive him of his source of income entirely. In other words, the uncertainties of a free market regime can serve, to some extent at least, as a surrogate for the veil of ignorance. To that extent the veil can be dispensed with.

Is it then simply rational for everyone to agree to a state-guaranteed social minimum? Not exactly – this still depends on attitudes to risk, as does the level of the minimum (and concomitant redistribution) that it would be rational to choose. These attitudes vary from person to person, and from society to society. Nevertheless, we can still defend a *modest* hypothetical contractualism; a contractualism much more modest than traditional contract theory in the following ways. Firstly, in so far as it derives specific conclusions, it must be admitted that these will be applicable only to particular societies, not universally. For example, only for societies where *economic security* is relatively highly valued will the contractarian argument yield support for a social minimum.

Secondly, the conclusions cannot be *too* specific – thus, even in a society in which people value economic security, not everyone puts the same value on it, and so there is no single level of social minimum that can reflect everyone's attitude. And thirdly, there are likely to be some people, even in such a security-minded society, whose attitudes to risk are so positive that, for them, acceptance of a social minimum is not rational at all. In sum, this modest contractualism can hope to be persuasive only to the great bulk of members of particular societies (not to all members of all societies), and can only lay down rather general prescriptions. Thus, a social contract argument applied to the countries of Western Europe in the late twentieth century – societies where economic security *is* highly valued – can be used to justify a relatively generous social minimum, but not at any specific level, and certainly not the 'maximum minimum' prescribed by Rawls. In the USA, perhaps, attitudes to risk are more positive, the desire for security less strong and widespread, and for that country 'modest' contractarianism prescribes a less generous minimum, or even conceivably none at all.

This modest contractualism does not solve the problems that beset social contract theory in its various forms, but suggests what it can achieve nevertheless – and also the limitations thereof. What has just been established is that, in a society that values economic security, individuals in general (if not absolutely every individual) have good reason to prefer some level of minimum income guarantee to the distribution produced by a completely unfettered market. This is not to say that there is any specific level which is optimum for all, and which all should prefer; there is not. Now, there is a significant parallel between this argument for social security, and the traditional contractarian argument for government; the latter is, one might say, essentially that government makes life *more secure* (less risky) than in the state of nature – an argument compelling only to those who value security. There is, in other words, a formal similarity between the state of nature and the unregulated free market (which is *not* to agree with C. B. Macpherson that the contractarian argument of Hobbes *presupposes* such a free market) – both are highly risky situations in which men may seek security by setting up appropriate institutions. If, indeed, we may designate the market as natural – which it presumably is, in the sense of evolving spontaneously, rather than as a result of deliberate design – then such a free market can be considered analogous to the state of nature in a further sense, or even as part of a (hypothetical) state of nature. Just as a completely unregulated free market would be a predicament from which men would very likely wish to escape, but we cannot say exactly to what, so the same is true of the state of nature; we may plausibly argue that they would prefer government, but we cannot say exactly what system of government – whether Hobbes's, Locke's, Rousseau's, or Rawls's.

Even with this modest and rather unspecific contractualism a problem remains. If government is in the interest of (almost) everyone, by comparison with a state of nature, and if a scheme of social security is in the interest of (almost) everyone, by comparison with a totally free market, then this is no doubt a good argument for government, and for modifying the market to provide social security. That an institution benefits everyone, and therefore could be the object of a hypothetical contract, is sufficient to justify it. But it is not *necessary*, as we saw above (pp.128,130). Despite Nozick, it may perfectly well be justified deliberately to redistribute benefits; it may perfectly well be justified to redistribute from the well-endowed to the less well-endowed, against the interests of the former, or to establish government even if, for brave and skilful ruffians, a state of nature would be preferable (nor is it necessarily decisive how numerous the losers are compared to the gainers). It was, perhaps, precisely to deal with this problem that Rawls added the famous veil of ignorance to his contractarian construction, in an effort to enforce impartiality on his contractors. This veil, it seems, is needed to make the contract morally acceptable; yet, as we have seen, it also seems to create insoluble problems, by turning it into a case of decision-making under uncertainty, where the decision-makers have no knowledge of their attitudes to risk.

Can this dilemma be solved? I believe that it can at least be alleviated, within the terms of what I have called modest contractarianism – that is, a contractarianism that claims applicability, not universally, but only to particular societies, taken (so to speak) one at a time. To such a contractarianism we can apply a suggestion made in an article by D. C. Mueller, R. D. Tollison and T. D. Willett, which is directed to the problem raised for Rawls's theory by Harsanyi's derivation of utilitarianism from more-or-less Rawlsian premises. Harsanyi, we recall, argued that a rational self-interested chooser of social principles who is equally likely to occupy any social position should concern himself with the average utility from all social positions. Mueller, Tollison and Willett suggest a different kind of averaging (Mueller *et al.*, 1973–4, p.350). Rawls's veil of ignorance is supposed to make his contractors impartial in regard to, *inter alia*, different attitudes to risk; the suggestion of Mueller *et al.* is to lift the veil of ignorance just enough to allow them to know the *distribution of attitudes to risk in their own society* (that is, among the parties to the hypothetical contract), and hence to choose on the basis of the average degree of risk-averseness among its members. This proposal is in the spirit of our 'modest' contractarianism, in so far as it applies to specific societies, and also takes account of differences within them. And there is a further bonus: it makes 'modest' contractarianism a little less modest, by making its conclusions more specific. If we apply the idea to a society whose members tend to value security, we will get a definite and positive degree of risk-averseness which leads, in a way that is impartial as between different members of society, to a definite social minimum. The generation of this social minimum from a contract incorporating a near-Rawlsian veil of ignorance seems to remove the problem of even modest contractarianism noted above.

Thus, a modest contractarianism incorporating a modified veil of ignorance seems workable. It can, perhaps, be taken further. It might be used, for example, to ground the Rawlsian basic liberties (though not necessarily their priority); that is, a hypothetical contract can be used to ground protection of these liberties, for societies which value them. This may sound like arguing in a circle – basic liberties should be safeguarded for those who value them, because they value them; but it is not. The argument escapes circularity through the distinction between values and the distribution of what is valued. Where members of a society, by and large, value liberty, the device of hypothetical contract plus (or including) a veil of ignorance yields the conclusion that (other things equal) what is valued should be distributed in a particular way. Whoever wants liberty is forced by the veil of ignorance to agree that everyone ought to have it. And liberty is significantly unlike wealth, in that it cannot literally be redistributed from one person to another. Thus, in a society of slave-owners and slaves, the latter have less liberty than free men, but the former don't have more (what they have is more *power*). One cannot therefore gamble on having more liberty in a slave society than a free one. So far as liberty is concerned, no one has anything to gain from unequal liberty.

But what about power? One is tempted to agree with Hobbes that all rational self-interested persons must seek to maximise their power, since power is just the 'present means' to achieve whatever they value – like Rawls's social primary goods in general. (In this Hobbesian sense, power actually includes liberty and wealth.) However, the temptation should probably be resisted, even if we confine the term to power in the narrower political sense; for of power (as of liberty) it is at least plausible to say that it need not benefit its possessor, if (for example) he is sufficiently incompetent. To wish to exercise power, perhaps, requires some degree of confidence in one's abilities. What is by definition desired by a rational self-interested person is to maximise the benefit accruing to him from the exercise of power; under certain circumstances this will amount to maximising his own power, but not in all.

Let us explore the implications of this. We assume, as suggested above, that the modest theory of social contract suggests that government is necessary. If that is accepted, some distribution of political power is also necessary. Now, in an original position or state of nature incorporating a veil of ignorance, the old dilemma seems to re-assert itself: whether to maximise the average benefit from political power, or the minimum benefit, or something in between. But, by hypothesis (the hypothesis of modest contractarianism), we assume that our contractors value security (otherwise they wouldn't want government at all). Hence we have a contractarian argument for the usual liberal-democratic safeguards against abuse of power, and for a share in its exercise by ordinary citizens, for example, through representative institutions. Exactly how, and to what extent, the desire to safeguard benefits from political power translates into the claim to share in that power depends, among other things, on the political self-confidence of members of society, as explained above. It is worth mentioning, here again, that the argument proposed is not circular; we are not saying that for those who value the exercise of political power it is a good, and that therefore they should have it. Rather the point of the (modest) contractarian argument, again, is that what is generally valued (in this case power) must be distributed in a particular way.

If the foregoing argument has any merit, it suggests that a modest hypothetical contractualism is not useless. We may use it to think about our own society, at least if our society exhibits a significant degree of consensus on values. I suggest that it does. Our attitudes to security, both physical and economic, to liberty and to the exercise of power are sufficiently similar to ground certain, rather general conclusions about their distribution. If it is permissible, as suggested by Mueller *et al.*, to base a contractualist argument on the *average* attitude of our society in these matters, more specific conclusions can be derived. Broadly speaking, these conclusions constitute a justification of the political institutions of liberal democracy, the free market, and the welfare state.

8 Conclusion

Despite earlier obituaries, the history of social contract theory seems, after all, to be by no means over. Not only is Rawls continuing to refine his own theory; his work has also stimulated a considerable outburst of contractarian theorising, notably in the field of moral (as distinct from political) philosophy.[1] Despite its interest, this material has rather the character of work in progress, and is in any case somewhat tangential to our central theme in this book; so discussion of it would take us too far afield. Equally, the account given in this book of the past history of contract theory has had to be selective, and much that might have been included has been omitted, or relegated to the endnotes.

Nevertheless, one thing that I hope has become clear is that social contract theory has a genuine *history* or (to be slightly pompous) is a genuine historical subject; the subject of a process of change and development in which, nevertheless, sufficient continuity is evident to preserve the identity of the changing subject. We are talking, of course, of intellectual history, and our subject is an idea, or a complex of ideas – in brief, the idea of deriving conclusions about the norms of political society from premises about a contract (or contracts). It is indeed striking to what an extent early formulations of this idea have persisted even in later, innovatory versions of it. Thus, the medieval idea of a contract between ruler and people, initiated by Manegold of Lautenbach, and which became with Engelbert of Volkersdorf a theory of the origin of government, was repeated again by the radical theorists of the Reformation and still incorporated as a part of the revolutionary Calvinist contract theory of the *Vindiciae contra Tyrannos*. The second great Calvinist contract theory, that of Althusius, could almost be said to subsume all previous contract theory within itself, for it postulated an original contract between

158

people and ruler (Engelbert), a general contract between them (Manegold), and the characteristically Calvinist contract with God, as well as using, in its own peculiar way, the idea of Salamonio that a political society is governed by laws agreed by those who make it up, and who established it. The debt of Hobbes, Pufendorf, Locke, Rousseau and Kant to their respective predecessors, and ultimately therefore to Althusius, is too obvious to need stressing – and not least where they were at pains to repudiate those predecessors, yet still remained within the framework of contractarian thought. Indeed, it may be said that the theories of Rousseau and especially of Kant, with their ideal versions of the contract, take the form that they do only because these thinkers were so deeply immersed in the contractarian way of thinking that this form was more or less inevitable for them, even although it was, logically speaking, not particularly appropriate.

Between the time of Kant and the modern revival due, above all, to John Rawls, there was a hiatus in a chronological sense. But it is a peculiarity of intellectual history that the historical subject can survive such a hiatus, and so it has been in this case. Rawls explicitly looks back to, and draws inspiration from, his contractarian predecessors, finding much of value in them, yet seeking at the same time to amend and correct the weaknesses of this tradition. In my judgment he has been, in many ways, strikingly successful in this, and it may be worthwhile briefly to rehearse some of those ways. First, he has made it clearer than ever before that the contract is for him not a historical event but a thought-experiment. Second, he has, I suggest, at last found the right *subject* for contract theory – the problem of justice. For what is intuitively attractive about the contractarian idea – at least in our culture – is the way in which it promises equal protection to the (possibly conflicting) interests of all individuals. As I argued in chapter six, this is individualism, but not by any means egoism. Only to those to whom the interests of (some or all) individuals are unimportant, or who think that individual interests do not, need not or should not ever conflict, will Rawls's use of contract theory be unacceptable in principle. Thirdly, he has replaced the classical contractarian concept of a state of nature by that of a fair original position, incorporating a 'veil of ignorance'. For this latter, he has been much criticised, but I have argued (in the previous chapter) that such a device is necessary if contract theory is to allow for adequate *redistribution*, which any just theory – and not only a theory of justice – must do.

Rawls's original position has another advantage over the state of nature: it can subsume the latter, but the converse is not true. That is, we may, as a thought-experiment, pose to hypothetical contractors in the original position a choice between the state of nature and government in one form or another, or, more generally, between the existence of some deliberately contrived social institution such as a welfare state and its absence (that is, leaving economic distribution totally at the mercy of the market). It was by adopting such a strategy, in effect, that I was able to argue (at the end of the last chapter) that the problems inherent in Rawls's veil of ignorance, and in contract theory generally, can to some extent be circumvented, so long as the theory preserves a certain self-denying modesty. In application to societies like our own it can yield principles that support some of our characteristic institutions. Since both these institutions, and the theory of social contract, have developed out of the same Western cultural roots, this perhaps is not too surprising. Yet, in principle, the application of even modest contractarianism need not be confined to modern western society; it should be applicable to any society that recognises the need for a just resolution of conflicting individual interests. And if this is not quite a universal applicability, perhaps it ought to be.

Guide to Further Reading

The most important further reading for students of social contract theory is, of course, the original works of the great contract theorists themselves. From the *Vindiciae* on, these works were either written in English or are available in English translation, as indicated in the Bibliography. Salamonio's *De Principatu* has not been translated into English, but there is a modern edition with scholarly apparatus in Italian (see Bibliography).

There are surprisingly few books on social contract theory in general, and none is fully comprehensive. Most comprehensive is Gough (1957), but this was written before the latest phase in the history of the theory. Three excellent scholarly works, however, span the entire history of contract theory to the present: D'Addio (1954), Gierke (1934) and Riley (1982). D'Addio covers the period from the sophists to the Reformation in great detail, and with copious quotation from original sources, but unfortunately his Italian text has not been translated into English; Gierke covers in magisterial fashion the period from 1500 to 1800, though he does not confine himself to social contract theory (see also Gierke, 1939); while Riley offers sensitive commentary on the main contract theorists from Hobbes to the present day, and on the significance of contract theory in general. Some shorter surveys of contract theory may also be mentioned. Ritchie (1893) is a useful brief summary. So too are the Introduction to Barker (1947), and Höpfl and Thompson (1979), though the former, to my mind, exaggerates the importance for contract theory of St Thomas Aquinas, while the latter is marred by an ill-judged polemic against Gierke. A useful brief analysis is in Scruton (1982). There are entries under 'social contract' in the *Encyclopaedia of Philosophy* (by Peter Laslett) and the *International Encyclopaedia of the Social Sciences* (by Willmore Kendall). Berry (1977) perceptively contrasts two major critics of contract theory.

In addition to the above, material on contract theory and related matters is to be found in more general works on the history of ideas and of political thought. The best single-volume work covering the latter is Sabine (1963). Guthrie (1969) gives detailed information on the Greek sophists and their contemporaries. Lovejoy and Boas (1965) survey attitudes to the concept of 'nature' in antiquity, and have useful material on and from Aristotle, Cicero and Seneca. The period from antiquity to the end of the Middle Ages is covered by the Carlyle brothers' indispensable six-volume *opus*, *Medieval Political Theory in the West*, which gives very full summaries of a large number of writers, plus lengthy quotations from the originals. Volume I contains material on Seneca, the Christian Fathers and Germanic kingship; Volume III covers feudalism and the period of Manegold of Lautenbach. A very useful medieval source-book is Lewis (1974), while a more interpretative essay on the Middle Ages is Ullmann (1967). The sixteenth century is surveyed by Allen (1960), though to my mind he is unduly dismissive of the significance of contract theory in the period. Finally, mention should be made of Tuck (1979), a book which, while not actually devoted to social contract theory, analyses the development of the related concept of natural rights in great detail from classical times to Pufendorf, and contains much of relevance to our theme.

As for the modern period, there are of course numerous commentaries on the main contract theorists from Hobbes on – too numerous to mention here. In any case the first priority is to read the theorists themselves.

Notes

Chapter 1

1. Printed in *The Times Guide to the House of Commons, October 1974*, pp.300–1. Cf. also the Labour Party's manifesto for the election of February 1974, in *The Times Guide to the House of Commons, 1974*, p.307.
2. On social contract theory and voluntarism, see Riley, 1982.

Chapter 2

1. Manegold has been frequently quoted and discussed. See, for example, Sabine, 1963, p.241, and CIII, 163–6.
2. Discussed in Sabine, 1963, chapter 12.
3. For example, Honorius of Augsburg, whose views are given in Sabine, 1963, pp.236–7.
4. Cited in Ritchie, 1893, p.201. Another ancient source, Plato's *Laws*, reports that the first kings of three Greek city-states promised their peoples 'to refrain from making their rule more severe', while their subjects promised to obey 'so long as the rulers kept fast to their promise' (cf. Plato, 1926, Loeb Classical Library edition, p.191). However, Manegold could not have been influenced by this supposed instance of contract, since Plato's *Laws* was then unknown.
5. For examples, see CIII, 53–72.
6. See CIII, 34–9,150–2; Carlyle 1903, p.240–8.
7. Cited in Ullman, 1967, p.82. Rufinus also held that men, after declining from primeval innocence into a state of war, made a contract or treaty of peace (*foedus pacis*) by which they promised one another mutual aid. Though interesting, this contract is of only tangential relevance to our theme, since it is conceived as linking all men, not the members of a particular political association (cf. D'Addio, 1954, p.221–8).
8. Lewis, 1974, pp.157–8; Gough, 1957, p.38; Sabine, 1963, pp.208f.
9. See Guthrie, 1969, chapter IV.
10. Plato, 1935, pp.36–40. A view similar to this seems to have been held by the sophist Antiphon (cf. Guthrie, 1969, pp.107–10, 138) and to have been revived in later centuries by Epicurus (cf. Gough, 1957, p.15).

163

11. It is of interest that the early Christian writer Lactantius apparently found it necessary to argue against the antinomian conclusions usually drawn in the ancient world from the idea that laws originated as contracts, and did so by invoking the premise of social contract theory – if cities did originate in compacts entered into for mutual protection, it would be highly wicked to violate this compact. But Lactantius does not actually believe that this was the origin of political life (Gough, 1957, p.20).

12. The *De Inventione* is cited in Tuck, 1979, p.33; the *Pro Sestio* by Lovejoy and Boas, 1965, pp.243–4.

13. According to the translation of Lovejoy and Boas, 1965, Cicero considered man's early savage state to be 'the condition of nature'; but in fact, Cicero says merely that the savage state was once how things were – '*natura rerum*'. Tuck, 1979, attributes to Cicero a similar view of 'the natural life of man', again without warrant in the text cited. Guthrie, 1969, likewise attributes to Protagoras (p.68) the view that the early savage state was a 'state of nature', but no such term is to be found in the passages he summarises. Sabine, 1963, even attributes the concept of a primitive 'state of nature' to Plato (p.78), but without any warrant that I can see. It seems as if even these eminent scholars have fallen into the trap of reading the ancient texts through spectacles fashioned out of later concepts.

14. See, for example, Carlyle, 1903, pp.23,127. Carlyle rather oddly claims that in Seneca's Golden Age there is no coercive government, while admitting that in it rulers exist who can expel dissidents from their territory. His interpretation is followed in Sabine, 1963, p.178.

15. Augustine, 1972, p.874.

16. Cf. Carlyle, 1903, chapters X and XI. See in particular the views of 'Ambrosiaster' summarised on p.113.

17. Carlyle, 1903, p.129. Presumably on this view the Fall did not bring about its full degenerative effects at once, otherwise the existence of the pre-political society would scarcely have been possible.

18. Cf. D'Addio, 1954, p.189. One such thinker is Nicholas of Cusa in the fifteenth century: 'Since by nature all are free, every government ... is based on agreement alone and the consent of the subjects ... By a general compact human society has agreed to obey its kings . . .' (cited in Lewis, 1974, p.192).

    Another major example is the late fourteenth century theologian William of Ockham, who also represents a type of contract theory on which this book does not dwell, but which deserves some mention – namely, a theory which postulates a contract as the basis of political obligation, but without drawing any specific conclusion from the postulate. Thus, Ockham noted that 'Augustine says, "There is assuredly a general compact of human society to obey its kings"', and some interpret this to mean that 'the emperor ought to be obeyed in temporal matters generally, so that he can command all things not contrary to divine and natural law'; while others hold that 'there is a general pact of human society to obey its kings in those things that tend to the common good', so that the obligation of obedience is limited to 'those things that further the common good' (cited in Lewis, 1974, pp.305,308). Either interpretation, it seems, is possible for Ockham.

19. At least one of the classical Roman lawyers, Ulpian, already took this view of the *ius naturale* (cf. D'Entrèves, 1970, pp.29–30; Tuck, 1979, p.34).

20. For the historical background of the *De Principatu*, see Skinner, 1978, pp.142–3, 148f. On Salamonio's contractarianism, see Gough, 1957, p.47 and Allen, 1960, pp.332–6. Allen misleadingly gives the date of the *De Principatu* as 1544.

21. Tuck, 1979, p.38, citing Salamonio's *Commentarioli*.

22. Ibid.

23. Notably Gough, 1957, p.47. See also GPT, 101–2. We saw above (note 7) that, in postulating contracts between free individuals, Rufinus anticipated Salamonio by several centuries – but with the crucial difference, from the viewpoint of political theory, that Rufinus's contract founds universal principles of human co-operation rather than the laws of the state.

Chapter 3

1. D'Addio, in his edition of Salamonio's *De Principatu* (S, 105).

2. On Calvinist covenant theology see Heppe, 1950, chapters 13, 14 and 16.

3. See GPT, part one, chapter 1, and F. E. Carney, Translator's Introduction to PJA.

4. On Mariana, see D'Addio, 1954, pp.473f.; Allen, 1960, pp.360f.; Gough, 1957, p.62; Figgis, 1897, p.108. Figgis, with justice, compares Mariana to Rousseau. Figgis and D'Addio may also be consulted on the use of contractarianism by other Jesuit writers; likewise Sommerville, 1982.

Chapter 4

1. Cf. Gough, 1957, pp.84–6; Höpfl and Thompson, 1979, pp.937–8; Ritchie, 1893, pp.213–14.

2. Cf. Woodhouse, 1938, pp.342–67.

3. Cf. Miller, 1982, pp.544f.; Höpfl and Thompson, 1979, p.942; Slaughter, 1981, p.330.

4. The account of Suarez is based on D'Addio, 1954, pp.459f.; Tuck, 1979, pp.54f.; Sommerville, 1982, pp.529–35; and Figgis, 1897. The interpretation of Suarez is much disputed (see for example Sommerville's comments on Tuck) but the account given above appears to be common ground among commentators.

5. Grotius 1901, p.63. Cf. also Tuck, 1979, pp.77–8. It may be somewhat

misleading to count Grotius as a contract theorist, since the unconditional alienation of rights which he considers legitimate is scarcely a contract in the sense we have adopted.

6. *The Elements of Law* was written in 1640, *De Cive* published in Latin in 1642 and in English translation in 1651.

7. HL, 183,81. The now canonical/phrase 'state of nature' is continually used by Hobbes in *De Cive*.

8. Hobbes is somewhat equivocal on the extent of the right of nature, apparently limiting it at times to what the agent judges conducive to self-protection. But the view of Tuck, that the limited right is the genuine doctrine of the *Leviathan*, is at odds with the balance of the text, and also makes it hard to see what significant renunciation of right is entailed by the Hobbesian contract. Hobbes's equivocation here seems to be an inheritance from earlier writers such as Digges.

9. The binding force in the state of nature of the third law of nature – to keep covenants – is another issue on which Hobbes is somewhat equivocal, sometimes suggesting, for example, that the obligation holds, *in foro externo* also, where one's contractual partner has already performed his part. This has led to much controversy among Hobbes commentators, but the issue is not of fundamental importance. It is clear that, for Hobbes, the institution of contracting could have little place in the state of nature, except to facilitate escape from it – and that *that* contract *is* fully binding.

10. For Hobbes's view of science, see HL, chapters 5 and 9. For the influence of geometry on Hobbes, cf. the famous account in John Aubrey's *Brief Lives*.

11. Moral obligation, too, is perfectly consistent with liberty, for Hobbes – thus the covenant of government is a 'voluntary act', though also an obligation of the law of nature.

12. Cf. the passage from Hobbes's *Liberty and Necessity* cited in Schochet, 1975, p.232.

13. Thus Peters, 1956, p.158: 'Hobbes did not take such a state of nature seriously as a historical hypothesis ... He was conducting a Galilean experiment of the imaginary sort – a resolution of society into its clear and distinct parts so as to reconstruct the whole in order of logical dependence rather than of historical genesis'. This, or something like it, seems to be the general view.

14. For Hobbes to say that there is no obligation not arising from the agent's own act, is an exaggeration because the laws of nature, which certainly oblige, do not so arise.

15. As in the famous interpretation of Macpherson, 1962.

16. Such seems to be the import of the widely influential view adopted (or once adopted) by Quentin Skinner (see Skinner, 1969, pp.3–53).

17. On Filmer, see Schochet, 1975, chapter 8.

Chapter 5

1. For Spinoza's political theory and views see his *Political Works*, ed. A. G. Wernham (London: OUP, 1958), esp. the editor's General Introduction, and the *Tractatus Theologico-Politicus*, chapter 16.
2. First published in 1672.
3. Possibly influenced by childhood memories of the havoc due to the Thirty Years War (cf. Krieger, 1965, p.13).
4. 'The social state is advantageous to man only when all have something and none have too much' (R, 181).
5. A recent commentator, Patrick Riley, has suggested that Rousseau remained fundamentally ambivalent in his attitude to the will of the individual, uncertain whether to repudiate it as the root of selfishness or to respect it as the basis of liberty (cf. Riley, 1982, p.16). Much that is obscure in Rousseau can, I believe, be traced to this ambivalence; but the dilemma that underlies it is an intractable one indeed, and a problem for all political and moral theory.
6. The Justice of Aragon is thoroughly discussed in Giesey, 1968, chapter 4; the institution is invoked in the *Vindicae Contra Tyrannus* (LDL, 179).
7. Cf. pp.13,34,37–8 above.
8. See above, p.82 (cf. K, 79f.).

Chapter 6

1. In chapter 4 of my *Structure of Social Science* (London: Allen & Unwin, 1974).
2. It must be admitted that Macpherson wrote many pages in support of this claim. None the less the whole argument is, in my judgment, question-begging (cf. Macpherson, 1962, pp.17–46).

Chapter 7

1. Strictly, utility-maximisation is not equivalent to self-interestedness. However, Buchanan and Tullock, despite some protestations, do not genuinely separate them. For example, they equate the 'utility-maximiser' and the 'profit-seeker' (B & T, 20).
2. *American Political Science Review*, 63 (1969), pp.40–56.
3. Rawls's defence of his position (see RJ, 161–83) makes explicit reference to Harsanyi's famous articles, Harsanyi, 1953 and Harsanyi, 1955. Harsanyi himself has criticised Rawls in Harsanyi, 1975.
4. Nozick stresses that economic freedom is incompatible with the achievement of any particular *end-result* or *pattern* in the distribution of wealth (N, 160–4). Hayek writes that 'a society of free men' cannot aim at 'a maximum of foreknown results' but only at an 'abstract order' that maximises for individuals their 'chance of achieving their different and largely unknown particular ends' (Hayek, 1976, p.114).

Chapter 8

1. Notable examples are Richards, 1971, Diggs, 1981, Diggs, 1982, and Scanlon, 1982.

Bibliography

Allen, J. W. (1960) *A History of Political Thought in the Sixteenth Century* (London: Methuen).

Altham, J. E. J. (1979) 'Reflections on the State of Nature', in *Rational Action*, ed. R. Harrison (Cambridge University Press).

Althusius, see Carney.

Anscombe, G. E. M. (1981) *Ethics, Religion and Politics* (Oxford: Blackwell).

Aristotle, *Politics*.

Augustine, St (1972) *City of God* (Harmondsworth: Penguin).

Barker, E. (1947) *Social Contract* (London: Oxford University Press).

Berry, C. J. (1977) 'From Hume to Hegel: the Case of the Social Contract', *Journal of the History of Ideas*, vol. 38 no. 4.

Bloch, M. (1965) *Feudal Society* (London: Routledge & Kegan Paul).

Browne, D. E. (1976) 'The Contract Theory of Justice', in *Philosophical Papers*, vol. V.

Buchanan, G., see MacNeill.

Buchanan, J. M. (1975) *The Limits of Liberty* (University of Chicago Press).

—— and G. Tullock (1965) *The Calculus of Consent* (University of Michigan Press).

Carlyle, A. J. (1903) *Medieval Political Theory in the West*, I (London: Blackwood).

—— (1915) *Medieval Political Theory in the West*, III (London: Blackwood).

Carney, F. S. (1965) (ed.) *The Politics of Johannes Althusius* (London: Eyre & Spottiswood).

Carr, S. (1975) 'Rawls, Contractarianism and Our Moral Intuitions', *The Personalist*, vol. 56, pp.83–95.

Coleman, J. S. (1976) 'Individual Rights and the State', *American Journal of Sociology*, vol. 82, no. 2.

—— (1977) 'Collective Rights *vs* Individual Rights', *Arizona Law Review*, vol. 19, no. 1.

D'Addio, M. (1954) *L'Idea del Contratto Sociale dai Sofisti alla Riforma* (Milan: Giuffre Editore).

D'Entrèves, A. P. (1970) *Natural Law*, 2nd edn (London: Hutchinson).

Diggs, B. J. (1981) 'A Contractarian View of Respect for Persons', *American Philosophical Quarterly*, vol. 18.

—— (1982) 'Utilitarianism and Contractarianism', in *The Limits of Utilitarianism*, ed. H. B. Miller and W. H. Williams (Minneapolis: University of Minnesota Press).

Figgis, J. N. (1897) 'On Some Political Theories of the Early Jesuits', *Transactions of the Royal Historical Society*, vol. XI.

Filmer, R. (1949) *Patriarcha and Other Political Works*, ed. P. Laslett (Oxford: Blackwell).

Fowler, G. B. (1967) *Intellectual Interests of Engelbert of Admont*, 2nd edn (New York: Columbia University Press).

Gauthier, D. (1977) 'The Social Contract as Ideology', *Philosophy and Public Affairs*, vol. 6, no. 2.

Gierke, O. (1900) *Political Theories of the Middle Age* (Cambridge University Press).

—— (1934) *Natural Law and the Theory of Society, 1500–1800* (Cambridge University Press).

—— (1939) *The Development of Political Theory* (London: Allen & Unwin).

Giesey, R. A. (1968) *If Not, Not: The Oath of the Aragonese and the Legendary Laws of Sobrarbe* (Princeton University Press).

Gough, J. W. (1957) *The Social Contract*, 2nd edn (Oxford: Clarendon Press).

Grotius, H. (1901) *Rights of War and Peace* (Washington and London: M. Walter Dunne).

Guthrie, W. K. C. (1969) *History of Greek Philosophy*, III (Cambridge University Press).

Hampton, J. (1980) 'Contracts and Choices: does Rawls have a Social Contract Theory?', *Journal of Philosophy*, vol. 77.

Harsanyi, J. C. (1953) 'Cardinal Utility in Welfare Economics and the Theory of Risk Taking', *Journal of Political Economy*, vol. 61.

—— (1955) 'Cardinal Welfare, Individualistic Ethics, and Interpersonal Comparisons of Utility', *Journal of Political Economy*, vol. 63.

—— (1975) 'Can the Maximin Principle Serve as a Basis for Morality? A Critique of Rawls' Theory', *American Political Science Review*, vol. 69.

Hart, H. L. A. (1967) 'Are There any Natural Rights?' in *Political Philosophy*, ed. A. Quinton (Oxford University Press).

Hayek, F. A. (1976) *Law, Legislation and Liberty, vol. 2: The Mirage of Social Justice* (London: Routledge & Kegan Paul).

Hegel, G. W. F. (1872) *Lectures on the Philosophy of History* (London: Bohm's Philosophical Library).

—— (1952) *Philosophy of Right* (Oxford: Clarendon Press).

—— (1975) *Natural Law* (University of Pennsylvania Press).

Heppe, H. (1950) *Reformed Dogmatics*, ed. E. Bizer (London: Allen & Unwin).

Herle, C. (1642) *A Fuller Answer to a Treatise Written by Doctor Ferne* (London).

Hobbes, T. (1949) *De Cive or the Citizen* (New York: Appleton-Century-Crofts).

—— (1968) *Leviathan* (Harmondsworth: Penguin).

Honderich, T. (1975) 'The Use of the Basic Proposition of a Theory of Justice', *Mind*, Vol. 84.

Höpfl, H. and M. P. Thompson (1979) 'The History of Contract as a Motif in Political Thought', *American Historical Review*, vol. 84.

Hoy, J. B. (1981) 'Hegel's Critique of Rawls', *Clio*, vol. 10.

Hume, D. (1951) *Theory of Politics*, ed. F. Watkins (Edinburgh: Nelson).

Joseph, K. and J. Sumption (1979) *Equality* (London: John Murray).

Kant, I. (1977) *Kant's Political Writings*, ed. H. Reiss (Cambridge University Press).

Kenyon, J. P. (1977) *Revolution Principles* (Cambridge University Press).

Krieger, L. (1965) *The Politics of Discretion* (University of Chicago Press).

Laski, H. J. (1924) (ed.) *A Defence of Liberty against Tyrants* (London: Bell) – a reprint of the 1689 English translation of the *Vindiciae Contra Tyrannos*.

Lewis. E. (1974) *Medieval Political Ideas* (New York: Cooper Square Publishers).

Locke, J. (1966) *Second Treatise of Government and A Letter Concerning Toleration*, 3rd edn (Oxford: Blackwell).

Lovejoy, A. O. and G. Boas (1965) *Primitivism and Related Ideas in Antiquity* (New York: Octagon Books).

MacNeill, D. H. (1964) *The Art and Science of Government among the Scots* (Glasgow: William MacLellan) – a translation of *De Jure Regni apud Scotos*, by G. Buchanan.

Macpherson, C. B. (1962) *The Political Theory of Possessive Individualism* (Oxford University Press).

—— (1973) 'Rawls' Models of Man and Society', *Philosophy of the Social Sciences*, vol. 3, no. 4.

Miller, J. (1982) 'The Glorious Revolution', *The Historical Journal*, vol. 25.

Milton, J. (1974) *Selected Prose* ed. C. A. Patrides (Harmondsworth: Penguin).

Mueller, D. C., R. D. Tollison and T. D. Willett (1973–4) 'The Utilitarian Contract: a Generalization of Rawls' Theory of Justice', *Theory and Decision*, vol. 4.

Nozick, R. (1974) *Anarchy, State and Utopia* (Oxford: Blackwell).

Pashukanis, E. B. (1951) 'Theory of Law and Marxism', in H. W. Babb and J. N. Hazard, *Soviet Legal Philosophy* (Harvard University Press).

Pateman, C. (1979) *The Problem of Political Obligation: a Critical Analysis* (London: John Wiley).

Peters, R. S. (1956) *Hobbes* (Harmondsworth: Penguin).

Pitkin, H. (1965) 'Obligation and Consent I', *American Political Science Review*, vol. 59.

—— (1966) 'Obligation and Consent II', *American Political Science Review*, vol. 60.

Plato (1926) *The Laws* (Loeb Classical Library, London: Heinemann).

—— (1935) *The Republic* (London: Dent).

—— (1959) *The Last Days of Socrates* (Harmondsworth: Penguin).

Pufendorf, S. (1927) *De Officio Hominis et Civis* (New York: Oxford University Press).

—— (1934) *De Jure Naturae et Gentium* (Oxford: Clarendon Press).

Rae, D. W. (1969) 'Decision-Rules and Individual Values in Constitutional Choice', *American Political Science Review*, vol. 63.

Rawls, J. (1963) 'Constitutional Liberty and the Concept of Justice', in *Nomos 6*, eds C. J. Friedrich and J. W. Chapman (New York: Atherton Press).

—— (1964) 'Justice as Fairness', in *Philosophy, Politics and Society*, 2nd series, eds P. Laslett and W. G. Runciman (Oxford: Blackwell).

—— (1971) *A Theory of Justice* (Harvard University Press).

Richards, A. J. (1971) *A Theory of Reasons for Action* (Oxford University Press).

Riley, P. (1982) *Will and Political Legitimacy* (Harvard University Press).

Ritchie, D. G. (1893) 'Contributions to the History of the Social Contract Theory', in *Darwin and Hegel* (London: Sonnenschein & Co.).

Rousseau, J.-J. (1973) *The Social Contract and Discourses* (London: Dent).

Rutherford, S. (1644) *Lex Rex* (London).

Sabine, G. H. (1963) *A History of Political Theory*, 3rd edn (London: Harrap).

Salamonio, M. (1955) *De Principatu* (Milan: Giuffre Editore).

Sandel, M. J. (1982) *Liberalism and the Limits of Justice* (Cambridge University Press).

Scanlon, T. M. (1982) 'Contractualism and Utilitarianism', in *Utilitarianism and Beyond*, eds A. Sen and B. Williams (Cambridge University Press).

Schochet, G. (1975) *Patriarchalism in Political Thought* (New York: Basic Books).

Scruton, R. (1982) *A Dictionary of Political Thought* (London: Macmillan).

Skinner, Q. (1969) 'Meaning and Understanding in the History of Ideas', *History and Theory*, vol. 8, pp.3–53.

—— (1978) *The Foundations of Modern Political Thought, vol. 1: The Renaissance* (Cambridge University Press).

Slaughter, T. P. (1981) ' "Abdicate" and "Contract" in the Glorious Revolution', *The Historical Journal*, vol. 24.

Sommerville, J. P. (1982) 'From Suarez to Filmer: a Reappraisal', *The Historical Journal*, vol. 25.

Spinoza, B. (1958) *Political Works*, ed. A. G. Wernham (London: Oxford University Press).

——, *Tractatus Theologico – Politicus*.

The Times Guide to the House of Commons, 1974.

The Times Guide to the House of Commons, October 1974.

Tuck, R. (1979) *Natural Rights Theories: Their Origin and Development* (Cambridge University Press).

Ullmann, W. (1967) *The Individual and Society in the Middle Ages* (London: Methuen).

Williams, G. (1957) *Salmond on Jurisprudence*, 11th edn (London: Sweet & Maxwell).

Woodhouse, A. S. P. (1938) *Puritanism and Liberty* (London: Dent).

Index